# Futures Research and the Strategic Planning Process:
## Implications for Higher Education

by James L. Morrison, William L. Renfro, and Wayne I. Boucher

*ASHE-ERIC Higher Education Research Report No. 9, 1984*

Prepared by

 ® *Clearinghouse on Higher Education*
*The George Washington University*

Published by

*Association for the Study of Higher Education*

Jonathan D. Fife,
Series Editor

**Cite as:**
Morrison, James L.; Renfro, William L.; and Boucher, Wayne I.
*Futures Research and the Strategic Planning Process: Implications for Higher Education.* ASHE-ERIC Higher Education Research Report No. 9. Washington, D.C.: Association for the Study of Higher Education, 1984.

The ERIC Clearinghouse on Higher Education invites individuals to submit proposals for writing monographs for the Higher Education Research Report series. Proposals must include:
1. A detailed manuscript proposal of not more than five pages.
2. A 75-word summary to be used by several review committees for the initial screening and rating of each proposal.
3. A vita.
4. A writing sample.

**Library of Congress Catalog Card Number: 85-61908**
**ISSN 0737-1292**
**ISBN 0-913317-18-7**

**ERIC** **Clearinghouse on Higher Education**
The George Washington University
One Dupont Circle, Suite 630
Washington, D.C. 20036

**ASHE** **Association for the Study of Higher Education**
One Dupont Circle, Suite 630
Washington, D.C. 20036

This publication was partially prepared with funding from the National Institute of Education, U.S. Department of Education, under contract no. 400-82-0011. The opinions expressed in this report do not necessarily reflect the positions or policies of NIE or the Department.

# EXECUTIVE SUMMARY

America's colleges and universities are undergoing changes
as profound as those that transformed the nineteenth century world of small religious colleges into universities.
These changes are part of a larger transition in American
society—the transition into an "information age." Rapid
technological developments in computers and telecommunications are revolutionizing instruction and management.
Rapid changes in the workplace are causing adults to reen-
ter postsecondary education—to enhance their quality of
life and to obtain essential retraining. Many colleges and
universities are faced with retrenchment and budget cuts,
constricting finances, increased competition, changes in
the demographics and values of the student body, some
overflowing degree programs and others half full, and an
increased uncertainty among the public about the worth of
a college education. It is becoming more evident that traditional methods of long-range planning, with their inward
focus on budgets and staff, are inadequate for our educational institutions. Faced with much the same challenges,
the business sector over the past two decades has developed a body of concepts and techniques known as "strategic planning." This volume explains how and why institutions of higher education can exploit futures research in
strategic planning.

**What Is Strategic Planning?**
When augmented by futures research, contemporary strategic planning differs from traditional long-range planning
in that it adds a special emphasis on discerning and understanding potential changes in the external environment,
competitive conditions, threats, and opportunities. It attempts to develop a greater sensitivity to the changing
external world and assist the organization to thrive by cap-
italizing on existing strengths (Cyert 1983, p. vii). It is an
approach that gets key administrators "thinking inno-
vatively and acting strategically, with a future in mind"
(Keller 1983). Modern strategic planning recognizes that
organizations are shaped by outside forces at least as much
as by internal ones. In particular, it represents an effort to
"make this year's decisions more intelligent by looking
toward the probable future in coupling the decisions to an
overall institutional strategy" (Keller 1983, p. 182).
Clearly, success in this endeavor depends upon having an

adequate and effective means of identifying and forecasting what is likely to happen in the external environment and how these events may affect the institution.

## How Is Environmental Scanning Useful for Higher Education?

A planning model that has emerged from futures research can serve to enhance planning in higher education. This model, the "environmental scanning model," begins with scanning the external environment for emerging issues that may pose threats or opportunities to the organization. Establishing the capability for environmental scanning requires the naming of an in-house, interdisciplinary scanning committee whose purpose is to develop a taxonomy of issues that disciplines the search for important possible developments in the social, economic, legislative/regulatory, and technological environments. (Within these broad categories, more specific categories relating to the immediate concerns of the institution may be developed.) It also requires the identification of sources of information and their assignment to individual members of the committee. It is important that high-level administrators be on this scanning committee, as their broad perspective on the institution's current operations and likely future directions will be essential in evaluating the potential significance of issues identified during scanning.

Even an elementary environmental scanning system can quickly identify a plethora of emerging issues. These issues must be limited to some manageable number to ensure the organization's effectiveness. To limit the issues, the planning committee must address certain questions: (1) What is the probability that an issue will actually emerge? (2) Assuming that it does actually emerge, to what extent will it affect current strategic assumptions and plans? (3) What strategies are available to the institution to manage its resources in anticipation of the issue, and how effective could each of them be?

## How Can Environmental Scanning Be Used in Forecasting the Institution's Future?

Several methods are available to respond to these questions and thereby enable the institution to order the issues and then probe them in greater detail according to their relative importance. For example, if the "issue" takes the form of a series of events—for example, the elimination of tenure—the results of the first two questions can be plotted on probability-impact charts. That is, the planning committee's collective judgments on the events' probability over time and their impact can be determined through simple questionnaires or a meeting in which the group's opinions are quantified using various scales. These estimates can then be cross-plotted, which immediately reveals which events have high probability but low impact or low probability but high impact.

The next step is to forecast in detail the trends or events that make up the issues identified earlier. One of the most popular types of forecasting for harnessing the insights, experience, and judgment of knowledgeable people is the Delphi technique, which can be used to develop forecasts from a group of "experts," a process in which individuals forecast each trend and event privately, the results are synthesized by an intermediary, and the resulting summary is fed back to each member of the group with a request to reestimate the forecast in light of the results obtained. This process continues until the group's consensus is close enough for practical purposes or the reasons why such a consensus cannot be achieved have been documented.

Other forecasting techniques include mathematical trend extrapolation (such as regression analysis), time-series models (such as the Box-Jenkins technique), and probabilistic forecasts, which are distinguished by including the estimated probabilities and impacts of possible future surprise developments to adjust the extrapolative forecasts of a trend. Cross-impact analysis is an especially interesting type of probabilistic forecasting technique, for it enables the user to produce comprehensive forecasts by taking systematic account of the effects of the occurrence of a particular future event on each of the other events in the set being considered, as well as the event's effects on each trend in the set. Policy impact analysis is cross-impact analysis plus the ability to test candidate actions within the model—that is, to simulate their consequences. By repeating these simulations it is possible to develop a number of alternative futures, which can then be described by multiple scenarios.

These methods serve to enhance our vision of what lies in the future so that we can examine the practicality of our plans vis-à-vis these possible futures. Such forecasting methods, then, provide administrators with a much richer information base on which to establish goals, develop and evaluate alternative policies, outline programs to implement these policies, and design systems to monitor the effectiveness of the policies.

The field of futures research has always been controversial, and many academics doubt its legitimacy, particularly those who have been led to believe that futures research seeks to predict the future (which it does not), that it is a science (which it is not), or that it will somehow replace established research methods and concepts (which it cannot). This volume attempts to make clear that the approaches, the techniques, and the very philosophy of futures research have been developed to *augment* the capability of individuals and institutions to deal intelligently with uncertainty, change, and complex interrelationships. The theme of this volume therefore is that merging the environmental scanning model with conventional planning approaches will enhance planning in higher education. This argument rests in large part on experience with successful strategic forecasting and planning in other organizations: the military, private business, trade and professional associations, and the volunteer sector. Arguing from analogy is always dangerous, of course, but there is no reason why many of the lessons painfully learned in other sectors cannot be adapted to the administration of colleges and universities.

Indeed, many higher education administrators realize that the need for new approaches is growing. When they recognize that they already have a wealth of information about their institutions and about society and that techniques used in futures research can provide models for structuring and improving the quality of this information, they will be ready to adopt new methods to build their future.

*If we are to respond creatively, we must begin to look beyond our own organizational boundaries and anticipate internal changes brought on by changing external conditions. We must take our early warning signals, combine them with our existing internal data and forecasting techniques, and ensure that we tap the wealth of creativity and resourcefulness higher education has to offer* (Heydinger 1983, p. 98).

**Virginia B. Nordby**
Director
Affirmative Action Programs
University of Michigan

**Harold Orlans**
Office of Programs and Policy
United States Civil Rights Commission

**Lois S. Peters**
Center for Science and Technology Policy
New York University

**John M. Peterson**
Director, Technology Planning
The B. F. Goodrich Company

**Marianne Phelps**
Assistant Provost for Affirmative Action
The George Washington University

**Richard H. Quay**
Social Science Librarian
Miami University

**John E. Stecklein**
Professor of Educational Psychology
University of Minnesota

**Donald Williams**
Professor of Higher Education
University of Washington

# CONTENTS

# FOREWORD

If anything, the problems now facing higher education should have taught us the need for sound long-range planning. Many of today's conditions—the decrease in the population of traditional 18- to 24-year-old students, the deteriorating infrastructure of higher education institutions, the obsolescence of research equipment, and the stagnation of faculty—could all have been predicted five or ten years ahead of their impact. For many colleges and universities, even those with a long-range planning strategy, it was not the case, however. The reason is that much of the planning in higher education is based on the assumption that what has happened in the past will happen in the future; institutions would do better to try to anticipate events that might *differ* from the economic, social, and political conditions of the present.

The processes of planning over the past decade should also have taught that, for changes to occur within the institution to meet the changes of the external environment, the entire institution must in some fashion be involved in planning. Sudden institutional change is unlikely to be successfully or harmoniously accepted without the involvement of both administrators and faculty.

This report by James L. Morrison, Professor of Education, The University of North Carolina at Chapel Hill, William L. Renfro, President, Policy Analysis Company, Inc., and Wayne I. Boucher, Executive Vice President, ICS Group, Inc., addresses both issues: the development of a strategy to assist the institution in anticipating a changing environment, and a process that will ensure a smooth integration of the needed changes.

Morrison, Renfro, and Boucher propose the technique of environmental scanning as an integral part of strategic planning. They develop numerous techniques that, when used with an institutionwide planning committee, can help predict both threats and opportunities to the organization. Some techniques, such as the Delphi technique, are currently being used. Other forecasting techniques, such as mathematical trend extrapolation, time-series models, and probabilistic forecasts, are less familiar to higher education administrators, although they have been used for many years in the business sector. In many ways, this report details a revolutionary new aspect in long-range planning. But success will be determined by the institution's commitment to develop a planning process that ensures the involvement of the entire institution and includes a systematic reevaluation of its plans in light of unanticipated events.

**Jonathan D. Fife**
Series Editor
Professor and Director
ERIC Clearinghouse on Higher Education
The George Washington University

# ACKNOWLEDGMENTS

A host of colleagues who willingly gave large amounts of time and energy to provide feedback and criticize early drafts assisted the authors in this enterprise. We would like to thank George Keller (Barton-Gillet Company), Ted Marchese (AAHE), Robert Cope (Washington), Richard Heydinger and Jim Hearn (Minnesota), Marvin Kornblum (Congressional Research Service), Guy Siebold, Doug MacPherson, and Bill Haythorn (Army Research Institute), Paul Fendt, Bruce Sigmon, John Goode, Curtis McLaughlin, Tim Sanford, Pat Sanford, Warren Bannuch, and Sherry Morrison (UNC–Chapel Hill), Karen Peterson (North Carolina State University), Michael Marian (World Future Society), Lewis Perelman (consultant), Deloris Burke and John Rider (Duke), Jim Pierce and Linda Pratt (North Carolina Central University), Dan Ruff (Midlands Technical College), Phil Winstead (Furman), and Tom Mecca (Piedmont Technical College). The authors, of course, assume responsibility for the final product.

James L. Morrison, Chapel Hill, North Carolina
William L. Renfro, Washington, D.C.
Wayne I. Boucher, Harbor City, California

# THE RATIONALE FOR FUTURES RESEARCH

*A sense of the future is behind all good policies. Unless we have it, we can give nothing either wise or decent to the world.*

—C.P. Snow

A sense of the future not only pervades all good policies; it also underlies every decision of human beings. We eat expecting to be satisfied and nourished—in the future. We sleep assuming that in the future we will feel rested. We invest our energy, our money, and our time because we believe that our efforts will be rewarded in the future. We build highways assuming that automobiles and trucks will need them in the future. We educate our children on the basis of forecasts that they will need certain skills, attitudes, and knowledge when they grow up. In short, we all make assumptions about the future or implicit forecasts throughout our daily lives.

The question, then, is not whether we should forecast but rather whether we should articulate, discuss, analyze, and try to improve our forecasts. The premise of explicit forecasting is that by moving beyond our ordinarily unarticulated assumptions about the future, we can better guide our current decisions to achieve a more desirable future state of affairs. It is a matter of whether we will go into the future with our eyes and our minds open or stumble into it with them closed.

The process of forecasting and developing information about the future raises several fundamental problems. We know that we can know nothing with absolute certainty about the future. But we can know, in a weaker sense, a great many useful things about the future: when a contract is scheduled to expire, when an election is expected to be held, when a machine is likely to be replaced, when a new technology is likely to come on line, when the life of everyone who is over 40 today is likely to have ended, how purchasing patterns are likely to change if present social and economic trends continue, and so on. Knowledge in this weaker sense implies a possibility—sometimes high, sometimes low—that something may come along to upset our otherwise secure understanding of the future. When we grant the presence of uncertainty, however slight, then we are in the realm of forecasting. Forecasting is valuable and important even when we have less confidence. Indeed, it is

*The question . . . is not whether we should forecast but rather whether we should . . . try to improve our forecasts.*

often far more important and/or valuable to focus on those areas where our confidence is low and where uncertainty—and the likelihood of upset—are high.

Highly likely and highly unlikely events are not usually very interesting, unless, of course, they fail to turn out as expected. The "interesting future" includes such possibilities, but it also (and more importantly) includes developments of middling probability whose occurrence or nonoccurrence will surely be decided within the period of interest as a result of decisions and policies implemented between now and then. In a society and a culture based on the scientific process of experimenting to develop and prove what is or can be known about nature, the process of thinking about the future and making forecasts stands alone in its vulnerability. Yet in spite of these risks and the unpredictability of the future, we all constantly make assumptions about the future in guiding our everyday decisions. Occasionally, of course, our assumptions are wrong, and we are surprised by sudden opportunities or developments that create both pain and loss. Nevertheless, as long as the future remains unpredictable, we have no choice but to go on making the best, most reliable assumptions and forecasts about the future we can.

Forecasting and the study of the future raise another major problem. Individual reputations, especially in the academic world, are built on research that follows established rules and procedures, research that should lead to the same results, regardless of the individual conducting the research. Information about the future, however, is based on assumptions about which reasonable persons can and do differ. The information we generate about the future is fundamentally linked to our personal values, concepts, ideas, experience, outlook, and makeup. While forecasting and futures research have to some extent borrowed detailed research methods and scientific concepts from other disciplines, these procedures cannot change the fundamental nature of information about the future. In the end, this information is based upon subjective judgment. As a result, for people whose lives, reputations, and careers rest on successful adherence to the traditional established rules and procedures of research, making forecasts is uncomfortable, even threatening. To speculate about the unknown and the unknowable is to challenge one of the keys to their success—careful use of "proper" research methods. By recognized standards of every professional discipline, even the best information about the future is unacceptable, because its foundation is subjective judgment and thus it cannot meet traditional scientific standards of objectivity, experimental verification, reproducibility, and so on. All information about the future may be judged inadequate in this light, but information about the future—*any* information about the future—is better than *no* information about the future.

What is good information about the future? Simply put, it is information that helps us to improve our current performance so that we can achieve a better future than would otherwise occur. Thus, total accuracy in the forecast cannot be the goal. By the time we know that the information about the future is correct, it *must* be too late to do anything about it. For example, if an air traffic controller watching two planes on a radar screen develops a forecast that the planes are likely to collide, we must ask, "What should we do with this forecast?" We can wait, watching the radar screen to see whether the planes do in fact collide and thus confirm the accuracy of our forecast. But by the time we know that our forecast was correct, we have a catastrophe. The forecast has value only if we use that information to avoid the undesirable future of the forecast catastrophe by directing the aircraft to safer courses. This principle is just as valid for large complex social systems: What should we do *now* to avoid the catastrophe of bankruptcy for the social security system 25 or 40 years hence? What should we do *now* to avoid the catastrophe of certain present trends in elementary and secondary education?

A forecast can be a failure even if it turns out to be accurate. The Paley Commission appointed by President Eisenhower in 1952 to study the long-term energy circumstances of the United States generated such a forecast. The forecast that it produced—that the country faced an energy crisis in the mid-1970s—turned out to be quite accurate. The forecast was a failure because it was not used to avoid that crisis. Thus, the key criterion must be that the forecast is used—*used* to create a better future. To be used, the forecast must be communicated to the relevant decision makers, and they must believe the forecast and have the resources to act on that information. Naturally, the accuracy of previous forecasts derived from similar methods or produced by similar forecasters or forecasting groups would enhance credibility; that is, decision makers will be more likely to assume a method (or forecast) is credible if it has been accurate in the past.

Most of the forecasting we do is implicit—unarticulated—and can appropriately stay that way. Some of the forecasting, however, should be articulated, discussed, debated, evaluated, challenged, changed, modified, and used as we make decisions in an effort to achieve more desirable futures. Forecasting may be both inadequate *and* better than ignorance of possible futures. The curse of Cassandra was to know the future but be powerless to change it. Forecasting gives us our best information about the future, but we will never know the future nor the curse of Cassandra—for we have the power to change the future.

# THE STRATEGIC PLANNING PROCESS

### Evolution of the Concept

In preparing his famous history of the Mediterranean, Fernand Braudel discovered that he was writing three histories concurrently. His first work followed day-to-day developments, recording the events and ongoing progress of the society. He discovered, however, that a second level of ongoing developments was apparent—the level of structural and institutional change. Braudel realized that much of the surface history, or the indicators of surface change, depicted on the first level were driven by and dependent on this second level. Today we would categorize unemployment as a key surface indicator, and we would give it much attention in our first history. Yet over the past decade we have discovered that other forces shape unemployment, for example, the structural and institutional changes that are occurring as we evolve from a manufacturing, industrial economy to a service economy. If we want to understand the shifting demand and mix of employment in the country, we must understand the dynamics of baby boom demographic forces, the changing family, and emerging personal roles. Interest rates, economic growth, government policies, and other surface factors alone cannot explain unemployment rates.

*Early forecasting and futures research methods focused on indicators and measures of surface change.*

Finally, Braudel discovered a third level of history—one derived and focused on individual attitudes, values, and beliefs. He argued that these forces bring institutional and structural changes, which in turn bring the changes in the surface indicators. These three levels—superficial, structural/historical, and attitudinal—can be recursive; that is, surface changes "cause" structural changes, which cause changes in values, which then cause changes on the other levels. Consider, for example, how reliable, inexpensive birth control affected society's sexual values and how these value changes affected school enrollments.

These three levels of history can also serve as a means for viewing the future. Early forecasting and futures research methods focused on indicators and measures of surface change, such as unemployment, inflation, economic growth, sales of automobiles, and housing starts. Most of our discussions of the future still focus on these surface indicators, usually using implicit forecasts. For example, on the first page of the *Wall Street Journal* every day is a historical chart of some surface indicator from which readers can derive their own forecast. This chart serves to establish the unarticulated, implicit forecast.

Given this view of the future, it is not surprising that futures research and forecasting developed and used a host of extrapolative methods in support of long-range planning focused on surface indicators. These methods included, among others, regression analysis, mathematical and judgmental trend extrapolation, Box-Jenkins, and rolling averages. The focus of this traditional long-range planning was internal, based on tracking and forecasting an organization's or a system's internal development.

As surprise developments continued to upset the forecasts and long-range plans produced by these methods, forecasters modified them to take explicit account of unprecedented new developments and external "surprises." While many of them were surprises on the surface, futures researchers began to increasingly include changing structural and institutional developments. Thus, trend extrapolation was modified to become trend-impact analysis, a probabilistic forecasting technique in which an extrapolative trend is modified by the occurrence of hypothesized external surprise events.

At the same time, models of large systems created through the method known as systems dynamics were modified to include similar external surprises; with this modification, it became known as probabilistic systems dynamics. Relationships among external surprise events were also explored through such methods as cross-impact analysis. Most recently, in the mid-1970s, a method for guiding the development of responses to information about the future on the first two levels was developed—policy impact analysis. While a small scan of the external environment usually was made to identify candidate surprise events, the focus remained on the trends and issues developed from the traditional, internal perspective.

Today, methods are used that will take account of information from the third level of the future—changing values and attitudes. But these methods are in their infancy in this sort of application, and their users frequently have no clear idea of what balance should be struck among potential developments on all three levels. Coping seriously with this question is one of the frontiers of futures research. While we could of course approach this question through opinion research, opinion research has been notoriously weak in forecasting for the simple reason that individual opinion about the future is much more unreliable than opinion about the present. But the real difficulty with polling is not that individuals are unreliable; it is that pollsters who have tried forecasting have aimed at predictive accuracy with "one-shot" estimates. That is, they failed to provide respondents feedback on the original judgment, thereby prohibiting their using that information to reflect on the initial judgments or the arguments behind them. Consequently, the polling technique is limited in obtaining that information useful for managing change and increasing our options.

As futures research and forecasting methods became less quantitative and more qualitative, the process of exploring and responding to changing social structure and values (the second and third levels of the future) was becoming more and more important. The traditional "fire fighting" mode of public relations was modified to include a planning or forecasting role in what became known as public affairs. This role was extended to include policy planning. Thus, it is not unusual to find on a contemporary corporate organizational chart a director of public policy planning, a position stationed philosophically somewhere between the traditional public relations/government relations/public affairs function and the corporate planning function. In some organizations, the policy planning function has been extended to include a director of public issues, who is responsible for anticipating and helping the organization to respond to emerging issues in the external environment. The new field of issues management emerged as public relations and public affairs officers recognized the need to expand the use of forecasting and futures research in their planning and analysis of policy. The merger of futures research concepts and techniques into public policy planning holds the prospect that administrators will eventually pay much closer attention to detailed information about the future on all three levels discussed earlier.

Currently the most common technique used for including more information about the external world from both the second and third levels (structural/institutional change and attitudinal change) is *environmental scanning*. As with earlier forecasting, environmental scanning focuses first on the surface indicators—derived from newspapers, literature, and periodicals—as signals of underlying change in the more difficult-to-understand structural and attitudinal levels. Although refinements in environmental scanning will have to be developed, this approach to long-range planning moves us into the strategic planning process.

### Strategic Planning

The word "strategy" comes from the Greek *strategos*, referring to a military general and combining *stratos* (the army) and *ago* (to lead). The primary tasks of strategic management are to understand the environment, define organizational goals, identify options, make and implement decisions, and evaluate actual performance. Thus, strategic planning aims to exploit the new and different opportunities of tomorrow, in contrast to long-range planning, which tries to optimize for tomorrow the trends of today (Drucker 1980, p. 61).

Most colleges and universities currently engage in long-range planning, but they can fruitfully augment that work by using the concepts of strategic planning and thereby enhance their ability to steer a course in a changing external environment. This section briefly describes the traditional models for long-range planning and environmental scanning and then shows how these two models can be merged to provide the basis of a strategic planning process.

Traditional long-range planning in its most elementary form is based on the concept that planning consists of at least four key steps—monitoring, forecasting, goal setting, and implementing—which are intended to answer these questions: (1) Where is the organization now? (2) Where is it going? (3) Where does it want to go? and (4) What does it have to do to change where it is going to get to where it wants to go? (Renfro 1980b, 1980c; see figure 1). Performing these activities is a continuing process that, for example, produces a one-year operating plan and a five- or ten-year long-range plan every year. The long-range planning cycle begins by **monitoring** selected trends of interest to the organization, **forecasting** the expected future of those trends (usually based upon extrapolation from historical data using regression analysis or a similar technique), defining the desired future by **setting** organizational **goals** in the context of the expected future, developing and

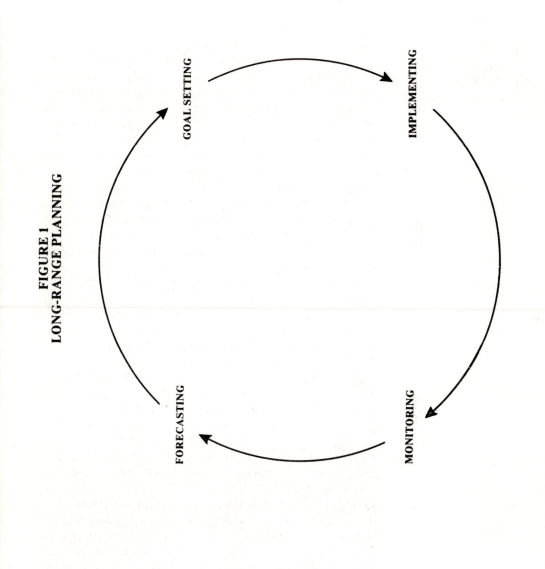

FIGURE 1
LONG-RANGE PLANNING

**implementing** specific policies and actions designed to reduce the difference between the expected future and the desired future, and **monitoring** the effects of these actions and policies on the selected trends.

The environmental scanning model (figure 2) begins with **scanning** the external environment for emerging issues that pose threats or opportunities to the organization. As part of this step, trends are specified that describe the issues and can be used to measure changes in their nature or significance. Each potential issue or trend is then analyzed **(evaluation/ranking)** as to the likelihood that it will emerge and the nature and degree of its impact on the organization if it should actually materialize. This stage produces a rank ordering of the issues and trends according to their importance to current or planned operations. The next stage, **forecasting,** focuses on developing an understanding of the expected future for the most important issues and trends. In this stage, any of the modern forecasting techniques may be used. Once the forecasts are made, each issue and trend is then monitored to track its continued relevance and to detect any major departures from the forecasts made in the preceding stage. **Monitoring,** in effect, identifies areas for additional and continued **scanning.** For example, subsequent monitoring may begin to suggest that an original forecast of the employee turnover rate is no longer credible, which would imply the need for more focused scanning, forecasting, and analysis to develop a more credible projection (see Renfro and Morrison 1984).

As noted earlier, one of the major limitations of the traditional long-range planning model is that information about the changing external environment is usually not taken into account systematically or comprehensively. When this omission occurs because of an assumption that "we cannot predict external changes," long-range planning destines itself to surprise and failure, if only because it locks itself to the information known from direct experience in the past and immediate present.

Information from the external environment adds important components to long-range planning, however. First, it identifies new and potentially crucial subjects that should be added to those identified and tracked during monitoring. Second, it identifies possible developments that must be used to adjust the forecasts of the internal issues derived

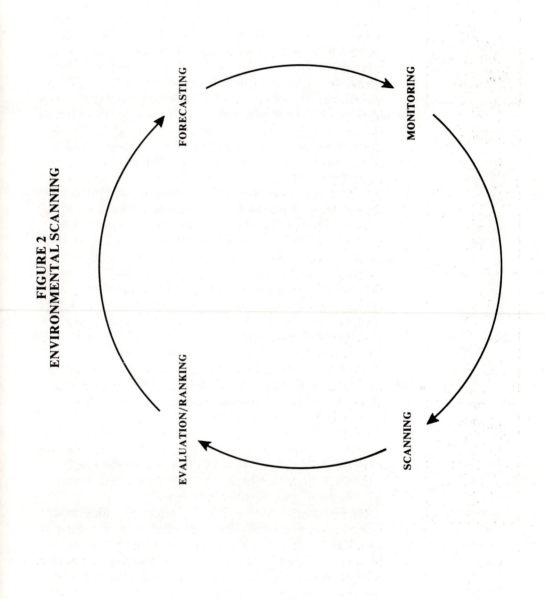

**FIGURE 2**
**ENVIRONMENTAL SCANNING**

FORECASTING

MONITORING

SCANNING

EVALUATION/RANKING

from forecasting—specifically, the surprise events that are used in policy impact analysis or techniques like probabilistic systems dynamics and in other rigorous forecasting methods used in traditional long-range planning.

These two models of planning—long-range planning and environmental scanning—may be merged. The interrelated model, *the strategic planning process,* consists of six identifiable stages: environmental scanning, evaluation of issues, forecasting, goal setting, implementation, and monitoring (see figure 3). The merged model, then, allows information from the external environment in the form of emerging developments to enter the traditionally inwardly focused planning system, thereby enhancing the overall effectiveness of an institution's planning. More specifically, it allows the identification of issues and trends that must be used to modify the internal issues derived during monitoring.

The argument for combining these two models becomes apparent when the future that happens *to the institution* and the future that happens *for the institution* are contrasted. In the future that happens *to* the institution (the typical "planned" future), new developments are not anticipated before they force their way to the top of the agenda, demanding crisis management and the latest fire-fighting techniques. In this future, issues are usually defined by others whose interests do not necessarily include those of the institution or its purpose. Not only are threats from the external environment not anticipated as early as possible; key opportunities will be missed or diminished in value.

In the future that happens *for* the institution, in contrast (the "strategic" future), administrative leadership is focused more on fire prevention and less on fire fighting. Hence, it is able to exercise more careful judgment in the orderly and efficient allocation of resources. Certainly management will still have to deal with unforeseen developments, but they will probably be fewer and less traumatic. Thus, institutions will be able to pursue their mission with greater confidence and consistency because they will be interrupted by fewer and smaller fire-fighting exercises.

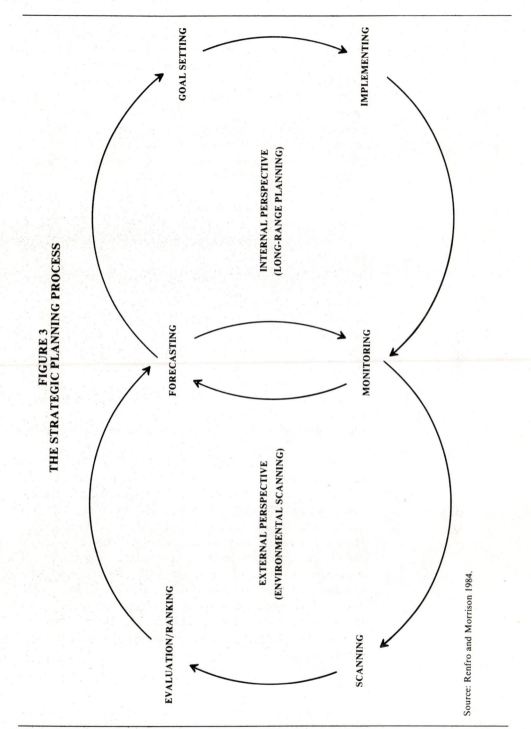

FIGURE 3
THE STRATEGIC PLANNING PROCESS

GOAL SETTING

IMPLEMENTING

INTERNAL PERSPECTIVE
(LONG-RANGE PLANNING)

FORECASTING

MONITORING

EXTERNAL PERSPECTIVE
(ENVIRONMENTAL SCANNING)

EVALUATION/RANKING

SCANNING

Source: Renfro and Morrison 1984.

# THE STAGES OF THE STRATEGIC PLANNING PROCESS

## Environmental Scanning

During the 1960s and 1970s, planners and forecasters succeeded in developing many useful methods based on an "inside-out" perspective; that is, it was implicitly assumed that knowledge about issues internal to their organizations was most important. At the same time, however, analysts increasingly found that emerging external issues often had a greater impact on the future of their organizations than *any* of the internal issues. In response, they began to modify some of their techniques and concepts so that outside developments could be formally included in their results. Initially, the emphasis on tracking the outside world fell on monitoring developments that, from an inside perspective, had already been identified as potentially important (Renfro and Morrison 1982).

Eventually, even this so-called "monitoring" was found inadequate as entirely new issues emerged that had major effects through mechanisms that had not previously been recognized. Thus, it became the responsibility of the forecaster to scan more widely in the external environment for emerging issues, however remote. The search for the possibility, rather than the probability, of major impact became common. The importance of scanning in the new sense was first recognized in the national security establishment and later by the life insurance industry, when it discovered that its market was declining. From the inside-out perspective of the insurance industry, the decline could not be explained. The economy was growing. The population was growing. The baby boom was just entering the labor market, adding millions of potential new customers. Yet the sales of life insurance failed to reflect this expected growth. Somehow the industry had failed to perceive a fundamental social change—the emergence of the wife as a permanent, second earner in the family. While many women in the past worked briefly before marriage or before starting their families, many if not most left the labor force when they began their families. In the late 1960s and through the 1970s, however, more and more women returned to work after starting their families. And this change affected the demand for life insurance: The life insurance needs of a family with one income are much greater than those of the family protected by two incomes. This development, coupled with a postponement of forming families, a decline in the birthrate, and an increase in childless couples, all reduced the traditional market for life insurance. That so major an industry could have overlooked these social developments stimulated the development of environmental scanning methods, particularly as the scope of scanning activities expanded to include technological developments, economic developments, and legislative and regulatory developments.

### Developing the environmental scanning structure

Two main barriers impede the introduction of environmental scanning techniques in higher education: (1) learning the new process and (2) achieving the necessary organizational acceptance and commitment to make the process work and be worthwhile (Renfro and Morrison 1983a). These two barriers pose several questions: How can an environmental scanning function be developed in an already existing organizational structure? How should environmental scanning work within the organization? What resources are needed for the process to function successfully?

While the organizational structure of the scanning function will vary according to a given institution's management style, the functions of the scanning process are universal. Developing a scanning function within an existing organizational structure is necessarily evolutionary because sudden organizational change is disruptive and costly. While the scanning function could be implemented in many ways, the most popular of the formal systems by far is through an in-house, interdisciplinary, high-level committee of four or five members (but no more than 12 or so). If assigned to a particular department or contracted out, the results of scanning can easily be ignored. And to achieve the widest appreciation of the potential interactions of emerging issues, the scanning function must be interdisciplinary. Without several disciplines involved, cross-cutting impacts, such as the impact of a technological development (for example, the home computer) on social issues (for example, the family), will most likely be missed. To facilitate the communication of the results of scanning throughout the institution, it is easiest to work directly with the various leaders of the institution rather than with their designated experts. Ideally, therefore, the chief executive officer of the institution should appoint the scanning committee, and to increase the likelihood that results will be incorporated into the decision-making process, the chair of the committee should be one of the president's or chancellor's most trusted advisors.

Perhaps the essential issue for the successful operation of a scanning committee is the selection of the other members. Ideally, membership should include a broad cross-section of department heads, vice presidents, deans, the provost, faculty members, trustees, and so forth. Certainly the institutional research office should be represented, if not by the director, then by a senior assistant. The objective is to ensure that all important positions of responsibility in the institution are represented on the committee.

High-level administrators should participate in scanning for several reasons. First, only those with a broad perspective on an institution's current operations and future directions can make an informed evaluation of the potential importance or relevance of an item identified in scanning. Second, the problems of gaining the necessary communication, recognition, and acceptance of change from the external environment are minimized. Hence, the time between recognition of a new issue and communication to the institutional leadership is reduced, if not eliminated. And when an issue arises that requires immediate action, a top-level scanning committee is ready to serve the institution's leadership, offering both experience and knowledge of the issue in the external world and within the institution. Third, one of the more subtle outcomes of being involved with a scanning system is that the participants begin to ask how everything they read and hear bears on the work of the scanning committee: "What is its possible relevance for my institution?" Indeed, the development within top-level executives of an active orientation to the external environment and to the future may well be as beneficial to the organization as any other outcome of the process.

A scanning committee does not need to have general authorization, for it serves only as an advisory board to the chief executive. In this sense it functions similarly to the planning office in preparing information to support the institution's authorized leadership. The scanning committee is, of course, available to be used as one of the institution's resources to implement a particular policy in anticipation of or response to an issue. But the basic purpose of the scanning committee is to identify important emerging issues that may constitute threats or opportunities, thereby facilitating the orderly allocation of the institution's resources to anticipate and respond to its changing external environment.

### The environmental scanning process

Environmental scanning begins with gathering information about the external environment. This information can be obtained from various sources, both internal and external to the organization. Internal sources include key administrators and faculty members; they could be interviewed to identify emerging issues they believe will affect the institution but are not currently receiving the attention they will eventually merit. Such interviews usually release a flood of emerging issues, indicating that the organization's key leaders are already aware of many important new developments but rarely have the opportunity to deal with them systematically because they are so overburdened with crisis management.

Administrators and selected faculty members could identify the sources they use for information about the external world—the newspapers, magazines, trade publications, association journals, and other sources they regularly use to keep in touch with developments in the external world. Typically, these surveys show that administrators read basically the same publications but only selected sections.

Scanning includes a broad range of personal and organizational activities. It is a process of screening a large body of information for some particular bit or bits of information that meet certain screening criteria (Renfro and Morrison 1983b). For example, some people scan headlines in a newspaper for particular kinds of articles, and when they find that information, they stop scanning and read the article. Then they resume scanning. This process has several distinct steps:

1. searching for information resources
2. selecting information resources to scan
3. identifying criteria by which to scan
4. scanning and
5. determining special actions to take on the scanning results.

How these steps are taken determines the kind of scanning—passive, active, or directed. (For an excellent discussion of scanning used by business executives, see Aguilar 1967, pp. 9–30.)

*Passive scanning.* Everyone scans continually. Whatever a particular individual's interests, goals, personal values, or professional objectives, it is an element of human nature to respond to incoming information that might be important. Ongoing scanning at an almost unconscious level is *passive scanning*. No effort is made to select a particular information resource to scan. The criteria of passive scanning are obscure, unspecified, and often continuously changing. Only ad hoc decisions are made on the results of this type of scanning.

Passive scanning has traditionally been a major source of information about the external world for most decision makers and hence for their organizations. The external environment has historically been a subject of some interest to most people, requiring at least passive scanning at some level for the maintenance of one's chosen level of fluency in current or emerging issues. The pace of change in the external environment has moved this scanning from an element of good citizenship to a professional requirement—from a low-level personal interest satisfied by passive scanning to a high-level professional responsibility requiring active scanning—more like the special scanning used for subjects of particular importance, such as career development.

*Active scanning.* The components of *active scanning* are quite different from those of passive scanning. For example, the searching or screening process requires a much higher level of attention. The information resources scanned are specifically selected for their known or expected richness in the desired information. These resources may include some, but usually not all, of the regular incoming resources of passive scanning. Thus, a member of the scanning committee would not actively scan magazines about sailing for emerging issues of potential importance to the university. This is not to say that such issues will never appear in this literature but that passive scanning is sufficient to pick up any that do.

*The basic purpose of the scanning committee is to identify important emerging issues that may constitute threats or opportunities.*

The criteria of screening for signals of emerging issues must be broad to ensure completeness, and they usually focus on certain questions: Is this item presently or potentially relevant to the institution's current or planned operations? Is the relationship between the likelihood and potential impact of the item sufficient to justify notifying the scanning committee? For example, a major renewal of central cities in the United States accompanied by high rates of inward migration might have tremendous impact on the educational system but just be too unlikely in the foreseeable future to warrant inclusion in the scanning process. It is not part of the institution's current "interesting future," which is a very small part of the whole future.

The interesting future is bounded by the human limitations of time, knowledge, and resources; it represents only that part of the future for which it is practical to plan or take actions now or in the foreseeable future. For almost all issues, this interesting future is bounded in time by the next three or four decades at the most, although most issues will fall in the period of the next 20 years. This time frame is defined as that period in which the major timely and practical policy options should, if planned or adopted now, begin to have significant impact.

The issues-policy-response time frame depends on the cycle time of the issue. For the issue of funding social security, the interesting future certainly runs from now for at least 75 to 85 years—the life expectancy of children born now. Actually, as their life expectancy will probably increase in the decades ahead, 90 to 100 years may be a more realistic *minimum*. For financial issues, the interesting future may be the next several budget cycles—just two or three years. For a new federal regulatory requirement that may be imposed next year, the interesting future runs from now until then.

The interesting future is bounded by a measure of the uncertainty that a particular issue might actually materialize. Developments that are virtually certain either to happen or not happen are of little interest in scanning, because they involve little uncertainty. If the institution has little ability to affect these more or less certain happenings, they should be referred to the appropriate department for inclusion in its planning assumptions. The aging of the baby boom, for example, is certain to happen and should be factored into the current strategic planning process. A potential new impact of the baby boom that may or may not happen—such as growing competition within the medical care system for federal resources—should be forwarded to the scanning committee for evaluation of both its probability and its importance. Thus, the interesting future is comprised primarily of those developments that are (1) highly uncertain, (2) important if they do or do not happen, and (3) responsive to current policy options.

A second dimension of scanning concerns the time element of the information source being scanned. Information sources are either already existing resources, such as "the literature," or continuing resources, which continue to come in, such as a magazine subscription. Passive scanning uses all continuing resources—conversations at home, television and radio programs, conferences, meetings, memos, notes, and all other incoming information. Passive scanning rarely involves the use of existing resources. Active scanning involves the conscious selection of continuous resources and, from time to time, supplementing them with existing resources as needed. For example, an item resulting from scanning continuing resources may require the directed scanning of an existing resource to develop the necessary background, context, or history to support the determination of an appropriate response.

*Directed scanning.* The active scanning of a selected existing resource for specific items is *directed scanning.* Usually this scanning continues until the items are located, not necessarily until the resources are exhausted. For example, if a member of the scanning committee knows that a good analysis of an issue was in a particular journal some time last year, he could examine the table of contents of all volumes of the journal to locate the article. As the specific desired item is known and the resource can be specified, the scanning committee can delegate whatever directed scanning is necessary.

### Scanning for the institution
To anticipate the changing conditions of its external environment, the institution needs both active and passive scanning of general and selected continuing information resources. The results of this process—in the form of clip-

pings or photocopies of articles—will be reported to the scanning committee for evaluation. The chair of the committee (or its staff, if any) compiles the incoming clippings to prepare for the discussion of new issues at the committee's next regular meeting. In performing this task, the chair looks for reinforcing signals, for coincident items (each of which may have sufficient importance only if both happen), for items that may call for active or directed scans of new or different resources, and for information about the interesting future.

*Developing a scanning taxonomy.* Any number of taxonomies and mechanisms have been used to structure the scanning process. All of them attempt to satisfy several conflicting objectives. First, the taxonomy must be complete in that every possible development identified in the scanning has a logical place to be classified. Second, every such development should have only one place in the file system. Third, the total number of categories in the system must be small enough to be readily usable but detailed enough to separate different issues. The concepts developed from technology assessment in the mid-1970s provide an elementary taxonomy consisting of four categories: (1) social, (2) technological, (3) economic, and (4) legislative/regulatory.

The taxonomy at the University of Minnesota, for example, includes five areas.* The *political* area includes the changing composition and milieu of governmental bodies, with emphasis at the federal and state levels. The *economic* area identifies trends related to the national and regional economy, including projections of economic health, inflation rates, money supply, and investment returns. The *social/lifestyle* area focuses on trends relating to changing individual values and their impact on families, job preferences, consumer decisions, and educational choices, and the relationship of changing career patterns and leisure activities to educational choices. The *technological* area includes changing technologies that can influence the workplace, the home, leisure activities, and education. The *demographic/manpower* area includes the changing mix of

*Richard B. Heydinger 1984, personal communication.

population and resulting population momentum, including age cohorts, racial and gender mix for the region, the region's manpower needs, and the implications for curricula and needed research.

To develop a more specialized taxonomy, the scanning committee should focus on the issues of greatest concern to the institution. The committee can use any method it chooses to select these categories—brainstorming, questionnaires, meetings, for example. Whatever method is used, it should be thorough, democratic, and, to the extent possible, anonymous (so that results are not judged on the basis of personalities). One method that meets these criteria is to use a questionnaire based on an existing issues taxonomy. Sears Roebuck, for example, has over 35 major categories in its scanning system, ALCOA uses a taxonomy with over 150 categories, and the U.S. Congress organizes its pending legislation into over 200 categories. Such a list can be used as the basis of a questionnaire that asks respondents to rate the relative importance of each category and expand categories that may be of particular importance to the institution. For example, under the category of higher education, the committee may want to add subcategories concerning issues of tenure and the academic marketplace, among others.

Alternatively, the committee may want to develop its own taxonomy. Although using a detailed taxonomy like the one Congress uses helps to ensure thoroughness and although an organized system can be adapted to new issues as additional categories are opened, the advantage of starting with only four categories is simplicity.

When the questionnaire is complete, the categories named most frequently should be selected for scanning. That number is determined by the size of the committee; experience indicates that a 10- to 12-member committee can handle no more than 25 to 40 assigned categories for scanning, with each member having responsibility for two or three categories and the relevant sources to scan for each of them. The list of categories then becomes the subject index of the scanning files.

With this list of categories and a list of the publications and other resources already being scanned, the committee can identify the categories for which assigned scanning is necessary. At this point, the kind of resource takes on

importance. For example, "alcoholism" may be an issue
selected for scanning but one for which no current resource can be identified. For this issue, generic and secondary resources may be sufficient—newspapers, national
weekly magazines, or other resources in the passive scanning network. Nevertheless, the resources designated for
this issue and their designated scanners should be identified. Of course, a particular publication or resource may
cover more than a single category, and it may take several
publications to cover a single issue adequately.

*What to scan.* Determining which materials to scan is an
extremely important and difficult task. This process involves deciding what "blinders" the committee will wear.
It is obviously better to err on the side of inclusion rather
than exclusion at this point, yet the amount of material
committee members can (or will) scan is clearly limited.
The decisions made at this point will determine for the
most part the kind, content, and volume of information
presented to the scanning committee and will ultimately
determine its value to the institution. This question de-
serves substantial attention.
   Because of the limitations of various resources, scanning
must be limited to those resources reporting issues that
have a primary or major impact on an institution, whether
the issues originate in the external world or not. A college
or university must anticipate, respond to, and participate
in public issues—issues for which it may not be the principal organization affected but for which it nevertheless has
an important responsibility to anticipate. It is useful, then,
to formally structure the discussion of issues and their
relative position to each other. An example of such a chart
is shown in figure 4. Such a chart creates an orderly structure for the discussion of issues, ranging from an introspec-
tive focus to a focus on the entire world. The levels should
be arranged so that all issues confronting the institution
can be identified as having their focus at one of the levels.
   The vertical dimensions of the chart are the areas of
concern to the university. Although they will necessarily
vary from time to time, the issues include students, research, finances, technological change, legislative/
regulatory change, social values, and more. The relative

## FIGURE 4
## CHARTING THE ISSUES

| | College | University | University System | State | Region | Nation | Western World | World |
|---|---|---|---|---|---|---|---|---|
| **Finances** | | | | | | | | |
| **Faculty** | | | | | | | | |
| **Students** | | | | | | | | |
| **Curricula** | | | | | | | | |
| **Technological Change** | | | | | | | | |
| **Legislative/Regulatory Regulations** | | | | | | | | |
| **Economic Conditions** | | | | | | | | |
| **Alumni Support** | | | | | | | | |
| **Sociopolitical Implications** | | | | | | | | |

importance of each of the intercepts of the horizontal and vertical axes can be evaluated using the Delphi process described in "Forecasting." For the most important areas—usually about 10 to 12—the next step is to identify specific resources to be scanned. An area that is ranked as among the most important but without acceptable scanning resources may require some additional research.

All members of the scanning committee should become more aware of their ongoing passive scanning. The special screen of the scanning criteria should be added to the flow of each person's continuing resources; it is a level of sensitivity that has to be learned with experience. It must be a rule of the committee that information in any form is acceptable. The process of passing notes, clippings, or copies from any resource must become second nature. The scanning coordinator or staff person will have the responsibility to process the incoming flow for the committee's formal review.

The committee must now address the question of the resources it will actively scan, and it must consider several aspects of the available resources in making the decision. First, a survey of the committee will show the specific resources included in its passive scanning. Then the committee must determine the kinds of resources it should be scanning, which involves the content and the kind of research—for example, germane to all issues, germane only to special issues, emerging or first impression of issues, the spread of issues.

In the process of assigning resources to issues, the committee should also address the question of the mix of the media it is using—from periodical to annual publications, from print to electronic forms—and it should review its resources to determine a balance in the mix of the media. A list of journals focusing on the general field of higher education or on specific aspects of the field is shown in Appendix A, and Appendix B includes publications focusing on external issues.

*Popular scanning resources.* Newspapers are a major scanning resource, and the members of the committee should cover four to six national newspapers to balance the newspapers' particular focuses and biases: the *New York Times* for its focus on international affairs, the *Washington Post* or *Times* for their focus on domestic political developments, the *Chicago Tribune* for its focus on the Midwest, the *Los Angeles Times* for its West Coast perspective, and one of the major papers of the Sunbelt. *USA Today* and the *Wall Street Journal*, with their emphasis on trends and forces for change, are perhaps the most popular newspapers of scanners. The national perspective should be supported by a review of the relevant major state, regional, and local newspapers.

Magazines, periodicals, newsletters, and specialized newspapers in each of the four major areas—social, technological, economic, and legislative/regulatory—should be included. But it is also important to include publications of special interest groups that are attempting to put their issues on the national agenda (Congresswatch, Fusion, the Union of Concerned Scientists, the Sierra Club, the National Organization for Women, and Eagle Forum, for example) and journals reporting new developments, such as the *Swedish Journal of Social Change* and *Psychology Today*. Although the list of scanning resources may appear formidable, the number of new periodicals added to existing resources may be quite small, for at most universities, some member of the faculty already sees one of the resources or it already is received in a campus library.

A special effort should be made to seek publications of the fringe literature—the underground press—as exemplified by the *Village Voice* and other nonestablishment publications. Depending upon the results of the survey of literature already being covered by members of the scanning committee, a special effort could be made to include publications like *Ms., Glamour, Working Woman, Working Mother, Family Today,* and *Ladies Home Journal*. Finally, the scanning literature should include a few wild cards— *High Times, Heavy Metal, Mother Jones,* for example. The scanning staffer should maintain a list of publications that are being scanned and the committee members responsible for scanning them. Ideally, each member of the committee should be responsible for three to four titles.

Additional resources for scanning include trade and professional publications, association newsletters, conference schedules showing topics being addressed and considered, and, in particular, publications of societies and associations involved with education and training. For example, many instructional innovations are surfacing in corporate training programs and are being discussed at annual meetings of the American Society for Training and Development and in trade publications like *Journal of Training and Development* and *Training: The Magazine of Human Resources Development*. As a further example, the forecasting movement and the concept of strategic planning developed in the business sector years before most individuals in higher education were aware of them as potentially affecting colleges and universities. Other industries— health care and social services, for example—may experience issues before higher education. Strategies for cost containment in the health care sector, for example, may well merit adaptation by higher education as funding support lessens (Morgan 1983).

A number of associations and societies track or advocate social change. The World Future Society, for example, publishes *The Futurist, The Futures Research Quarterly,* and *Future Survey,* all of which are dedicated to the exploration and discussion of ideas about the future. The American Council of Life Insurance in Washington, D.C., publishes a newsletter, *Straws in the Wind,* and periodic reports on emerging issues called *The ACLI Trend Report.* In addition, major corporations use commercial services to supplement their scanning functions: Yankelovitch's *Corporate Priorities,* the Policy Analysis Company's *CongresScan™* and Issue Paks, the Naisbitt Group's *Trend Report,* SRI International's *Scan,* and the Institute for Future Systems Research's *Trend Digest.* The more expensive outside resources are beyond the budgets of most colleges and universities and are not without their own liabilities (many of them attempt to cover all issues from all perspectives, making their results too general to meet the needs of specific organizations), and an overemphasis on outside resources violates an organizational requirement that the scanning function be developed within the existing structure rather than added on from the outside.

The scanning committee should make a special effort to include within the scanning process whatever fugitive literature it is able to obtain, that is, sources that are published privately and are available only if their existence is known and they are hunted down. Such literature would include, for example, the more than 25 articles, pamphlets, and other private publications now available on the new field of issues management compiled by the Issues Management Association in Washington, private publications on changing social values such as the 1981 Connecticut Mutual Life Insurance study, AT&T's *Context of Legislation,* and the publications of research organizations like the Rand Corporation, SRI International, or the Center for Futures Research at the University of Southern California. Fugitive literature often enters the established literature, but sometimes years after its initial private publication. Thus, it is necessary to develop personal and professional contacts throughout the scanning network to gain access to these materials. Professional associations like The World Future Society, the Issues Management Association, or the North American Society for Corporate Planning and their conferences can be major sources for fugitive literature.

*Other resources.* The scanning committee should tap the resources of its resident experts (Renfro and Morrison 1983b), best accomplished by the publication of a weekly or monthly scanning newsletter prepared by the committee's staff. This brief newsletter might present two to five of the more significant items recently found by the scanning committee. Such newsletters continue to build a constituency for the scanning process and an informal network for the recognition and appreciation of the results of scanning. The newsletter might be sent, for example, to all department chairs with an open invitation for their comments and for suggestions of new ideas they see in their fields. Colleges and universities are in a unique position to conduct scanning: Many organizations do not have the in-house experience that is available on most faculties.

Internal scanning newsletters frequently use political and issue cartoons found in major newspapers and in national magazines like *The New Yorker.* Such cartoons provide an important signal that at least the editors believe the issue has reached national standing and that some consensus on the issue exists for the cartoonist to create the foil and hence the humor. These cartoons serve the additional functions of communicating a tremendous amount of information in a very small space—a picture is still worth a thousand words.

After operating for a year, the scanning committee needs to review the clippings and articles collected and eliminate outdated materials. A staff person should have the responsibility of maintaining the files, opening and closing categories only with the approval of the whole committee. To keep the scanning from becoming outdated, the list of publications scanned should be reviewed and those resources that yielded little information in the preceding year dropped.

Operating an environmental scanning process requires a commitment of time and resources. It may be desirable for colleges to form consortia to share resources, following the example of the life insurance industry. Or they may develop cooperative arrangements with local corporations through which they receive scanning information, particularly projections of the region's economy and emerging technology. It is imperative, however, to establish an effective scanning system in this fast-changing world to identify as early as possible those emerging trends and issues that may so dramatically affect the organization's future.

### Evaluating the Issues

The most elementary environmental scanning system can quickly identify more emerging issues than the largest institution can address. Even Connecticut General Life Insurance Company (now part of CIGNA) limits itself to addressing no more than its six most important issues. The issues must be limited to some manageable number to ensure the organization's effectiveness. This limiting process is achieved by a rigorous, objective evaluation of the issues. The goal is to create a process within which the issues compete with one another to determine their relative and/or expected importance. The less important issues are the focus of continued monitoring and analysis or are used in the forecasting or other stages. The traditional methods of research analysis and forecasting can be used at this stage. Frequently, evaluation of the future impacts of an emerging issue must rest on opinion, belief, and judgmental forecasts. (Several techniques for gathering judgmental opinion as they apply to forecasting are described in the next section.) The methods described in this section for evaluating issues can also be used in forecasting.

### Probability-impact charts

One method of evaluating the issues, events, or trends identified during scanning involves addressing three separate questions: (1) What is the probability that the emerging issue or event will actually happen during some future period, usually the next decade? (2) Assuming it actually happens, what will its impact be on the future of the institution? (3) What is the ability of the institution to effectively anticipate, respond to, and manage the emerging issue, trend, or event? While these questions appear easy to answer, their use and interpretation in the evaluation process involve care and subtlety. The results for the first two questions are frequently plotted on a simple chart to produce a distribution of probability and impact. Many possible interpretations of the results can easily be displayed on such a chart.

The first question, that of the probability of the event's happening, may be easy to understand but difficult to estimate. If the scanning process has identified a particular event (that is, something that will happen or not happen in such a way that it can be verified in retrospect), then estimating the probability can be relatively straightforward. Suppose, for example, the United States replaces the current income tax system with a flat tax. This sharp, clearly defined, verifiable event is one about which the question being asked is clear (although opinions may differ). If, on the other hand, the scanning process identifies a broader issue that does not have this focus on a specific event, it may be extremely difficult to define when an issue has emerged and happened. In essence, the emergence of an issue is somewhat like news: It is the *process* of learning of something that makes it news. Thus, an issue emerges when it is recognized by a broader and broader spectrum of the society and in particular by those whom it will affect.

Collecting judgments on an event's probability, impact, and degree of control can be done by using simple questionnaires or interviews and quantifying participants' opinions using various scales (for example, probability can range from 0 to 100, impact from 0 to 10). When all participants have made their forecasts, the next step is to calculate a group average or median score. Quantification is useful because it is fast, and it tends to focus the attention

*What is the ability of the institution to effectively anticipate, respond to, and manage the emerging issue, trend, or event?*

of the group on the subject rather than the source of the estimates.

The next question concerns evaluating the impact of the emerging issue or event, based on the assumption that it actually occurs. Frequently a scale of 0 to 10 is used to provide a range for the answers to this question, where 0 is no impact, 5 is moderate impact, and 10 is catastrophic or severe impact. Usually plus or minus answers can be incorporated. This question and the first question (an event's probability) can be combined in a single chart that displays a probability impact space with positive and negative impacts on the vertical axis and probability from 0 to 100 on the horizontal axis. This chart can be used as a questionnaire in which respondents record their answer to the probability and impact questions by placing a mark on the chart with the coordinates of their opinion about the probability and the impact of the issue. When all of the participants have expressed their opinions, all of the votes can be transferred to a single chart to show the group's opinion. A sample chart with a group's opinions about an X-event and an O-event is shown in figure 5. The X-event shows reasonably good consensus that the event will probably happen and that it will have a positive impact; therefore, calculating an average for the group's response is useful and credible. For the O-event, however, the group shows reasonable agreement that the event has low probability of occurring but is split on its probable impact.

The X-event highlights one of the problems of this particular method: Respondents tend to provide answers either from different perspectives or with some inherent net impact where positive impacts cancel or offset negative impacts. In reality, an emerging issue or event often has both positive and negative impacts. Thus, the question should be asked in two parts: What are the positive impacts of this event, and what are its negative impacts? In rank ordering events, two ranks are prepared—one for positive and one for negative events—to permit the development of detailed policies, responses, and strategies based upon a recognition of the dual impacts of most emerging issues.

Even with the recognition of an event's dual impact, consensus may be insufficient to identify the average group response. In this case, it may be useful to return the

# FIGURE 5
## PROBABILITY-IMPACT CHART SUMMARIZING SEVEN VOTES FOR TWO DIFFERENT EVENTS

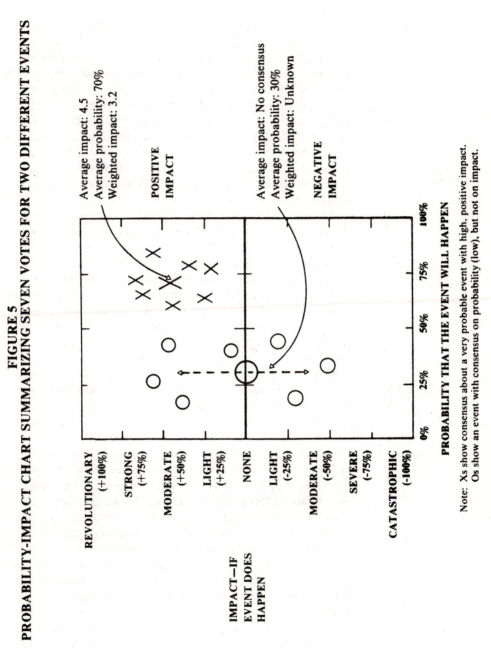

Average impact: 4.5
Average probability: 70%
Weighted impact: 3.2

POSITIVE IMPACT

Average impact: No consensus
Average probability: 30%
Weighted impact: Unknown

NEGATIVE IMPACT

**IMPACT—IF EVENT DOES HAPPEN**

REVOLUTIONARY (+100%)
STRONG (+75%)
MODERATE (+50%)
LIGHT (+25%)
NONE
LIGHT (-25%)
MODERATE (-50%)
SEVERE (-75%)
CATASTROPHIC (-100%)

0%   25%   50%   75%   100%

**PROBABILITY THAT THE EVENT WILL HAPPEN**

Note: Xs show consensus about a very probable event with high, positive impact.
Os show an event with consensus on probability (low), but not on impact.

Source: Renfro and Morrison 1983a.

group's opinion to the individual participants for further discussion and reevaluation of the issue. This process of anonymous voting with structured feedback is known as Delphi. Anonymity can be extremely useful. In one private study, for example, all of the participants in the project publicly supported the need to adopt a particular policy for the organization. But when asked to evaluate the policy anonymously on the probability-impact chart, the respondents indicated that though they believed the policy was likely to be adopted, they did not expect it to have any significant impact. This discovery allowed the decision makers to avoid the risks and costs of a new policy that was almost certain to fail. (The Delphi process is described further in the next section.)

When repeated reevaluations and discussions do not produce sufficient consensus, it may be necessary to redefine the question to evaluate the impact on particular subcategories; subcategories of the institution, for example, would include the impact on personnel, on finances, on curricula, or on faculty. As with all of today's judgmental forecasting techniques, the purpose is to produce useful substantive information about the future and to arrive at a greater understanding of the context, setting, and framework of the evolving future (De Jouvenel 1967, p. 67).

The most popular method of interpreting the result of a probability-impact chart is to calculate the weighted positive and negative importance—that is, the product of the average probability and the average (positive and negative) importance—for each event. The events, issues, and trends are then ranked according to this weighted importance. Thus, the event ranked as number one is that with the highest combined probability and impact. The other events are listed in descending priority according to their weighted importance.

Ranking the issues according to weights calculated in this manner implicitly assumes that the item identified in the scanning is indeed an emerging issue—that is, one that has an element of surprise. If all of the items identified in scanning are new and emerging and portend this element of surprise (that is, they are unknown to the educational community or at least to the community of the institution now and will remain that way until they emerge with surprise and the potential for upset), then the strategic planning process would do well to focus on those that are most likely to do so and to have the greatest impact

If, however, the issues are not surprises, then another system of evaluating and ranking the events and issues will be necessary. For example, if the entire community knows of a particular event and expects that it will not happen, then this low probability will produce a low priority. Yet, if the event would in fact occur, then it would be of great importance. The surprise then is in the occurrence of the unexpected. The key in this case is the upset expectation. It may be just as much of an upset if an item that everyone expects to occur does not in fact happen. Thus, the evaluation of a probability-impact chart depends on another dimension—that is, one of expectation and awareness. The most important events might be those of high impact and high uncertainty, that is, those centered around the 50 percent probability line. These are the events that are as likely as not to occur and portend an element of surprise for some portion of the community when they happen or do not happen.

Another aspect of emerging issues that is often evaluated is their timing, that is, *when* they are most likely to emerge. If an issue or event is evaluated in several rounds, consensus about the probability is often achieved in the early rounds. In the last rounds, timing can be substituted for probability by changing the horizontal axis from 0 to 100 to now to 10 years from now. Then the question becomes, In which of the next 10 years is the event most likely to happen? If necessary, additional questions can explore lead time for an issue's occurrence, year of last effective response opportunity, lag time to impact, and so on. All of these factors have been used to evaluate the relative importance of emerging issues and events.

Emerging issues and events that are ranked according to their weighted importance have a built-in assumption that should usually be challenged; that is, the ranking assumes that the administrators and the institution will be equally effective in addressing all of the issues. This assumption is almost certainly false and seldom of great importance. Suppose that the top priority issue is one on which the institution could have little influence and then only at great cost but that a lower-level item is one on which the institution could have a significant impact with a small investment of resources. It would clearly be foolish to squander great resources for little advantage, when great advantage could be obtained for a much smaller investment. Thus, in addition to the estimation of the weighted importance, the extent to which the event might respond to institutional actions of various costs and difficulty must be evaluated. The cost-effectiveness ratio measures the relative efficiency of alternative institutional actions—actions that are expressions of strategy. This outcome is especially evident when the differences in ratio are small, but if the emerging issues are competing for the same resources, the cost-effectiveness ratios will be essential in guiding the effective use of the institution's limited resources.

The top-ranked events may also be important to major administrative functions other than strategic planning. Many corporations, trade associations, and not-for-profit institutions have formed special "issues management committees" to support the authorized leadership of the institution in managing all of the resources they might have available to address an emerging issue. While such systems may be more formal than is needed at most institutions of higher education, they may serve as a useful model.

### Impact networks

Another simple evaluation method—the impact network—was derived from the concept of "relevance trees," which are essentially a graphical presentation of an outline of a complete analysis of an issue. Impact networks are a brainstorming technique designed to identify potential impacts of key events on future developments. An impact network is generated by identifying the possible effects of a given specific event. Such an event might be the abolishment of tenure, or the reduction of federally sponsored student financial aid, or the requirement that all professors be certified to teach in colleges and universities. When the issue has been selected and sharpened into a brief, clear statement, the group is ready to begin to form the impact network. The procedure is quite simple. Any impact that is likely to result from the event, whether negative or positive, is an "acceptable impact." The question is one of possibility, not probability. With the initial event written in the middle of the page, each first-order impact is linked to the initial event by a single line (see figure 6).

**FIGURE 6**
**IMPACT NETWORK**

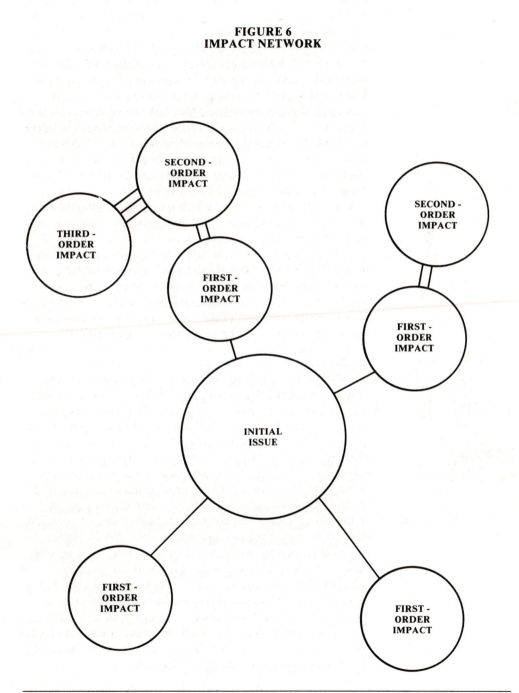

When five or six first-order impacts have been identified or when the space around the initial event is occupied, the process is repeated for each first-order impact. Again, the task is to determine the possible impacts if this event were to occur. The second-order impacts are linked to their first-order impacts by two lines. These steps are repeated for third- and fourth-order impacts, or as far as the group would like to go. Typically, third- and fourth-order impacts are sufficient to explore all of the significant impacts of the initial event. Usually a group identifies several feedback loops; for example, a fourth-order impact might increase or decrease a third- or a second-order impact. The value of impact networks lies in their simplicity and in their potential to identify a wide range of impacts very quickly. If more impacts or higher-order impacts need to be considered, the process is repeated.

A simple example of the use of an impact network illustrates the impact of the elimination of tenure in higher education (Wagschall 1983). As shown in figure 7, the immediate or first-order consequences of the event were perceived to be (1) reduced personnel costs, (2) more frequent turnover of faculty, and (3) an improvement in the academic quality of the faculty. Each consequence then becomes the center of an impact network, and the search for impacts continues. For example, the improvement of the faculty's academic quality causes improved learning experiences, students' increased satisfaction with their education, and the accomplishment of more research. The reduction in personnel costs produces stronger faculty unions, more funds for nonpersonnel items, and decreased costs per student. Increased faculty turnover produces a decrease in average faculty salary, an increase in overall quality of the faculty, and a decrease in the average age of the faculty. Each consequence in turn becomes the center of the third-order impact network, and so on.

A completed impact network is often very revealing. In one sense, it serves as a Rorschach test of the authoring group or the organization because the members of the group are most likely to identify impacts highlighting areas of concern. In another sense, by trying to specify the range of second-order impacts, new insights into the total impact of a potential development can be identified. For example, while an event may stimulate a majority of small, positive,

# FIGURE 7
# AN IMPACT NETWORK:
# THE CONSEQUENCES OF ELIMINATING TENURE

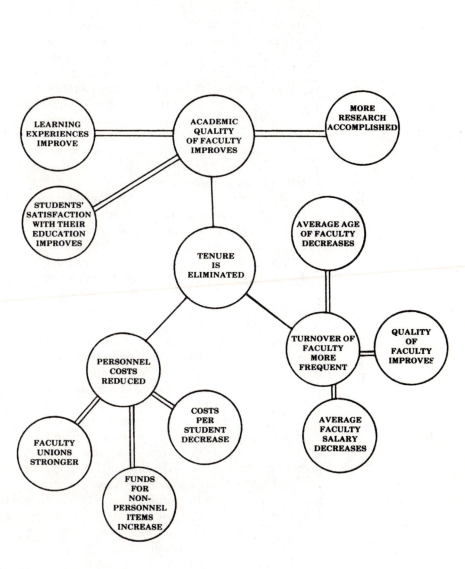

Source: Wagschall 1983.

first-order impacts, these first-order impacts may stimulate a wide range of predominantly negative second-order impacts that in total would substantially reduce if not eliminate the positive value of the first-order impacts. Feedback loops may promote the growth of an impact that would far outweigh the original estimate of its importance.

### Forecasting

Scanning typically leads to the identification of more issues than the organization can reasonably expect to explore in depth, given its limitations of time, money, and people. Simple evaluation techniques like those described in the previous section can help reduce the set of candidates to manageable size. The surviving issues can then be subjected to detailed forecasting, analysis, and policy evaluation. Many methods have been developed for forecasting. This section surveys the range of methods, beginning with several varieties of the simplest, most popular type of forecasting, individual judgmental forecasting. It then briefly describes techniques of mathematical trend extrapolation and group forecasting, cross-impact models, and scenarios.

### *Implicit forecasting*

According to Yogi Berra, "You can observe a lot just by watching." And much of what can be observed is the future. Despite the constant flood of assertions about the accelerating pace of change, despite endless warnings about impermanence and future shock, despite the vigor of the minor industry that produces one book or report after another that begins by telling us that we are on the verge of a societal transformation every bit as profound as the industrial revolution (all of which may actually be true), the present still foreshadows the future. If only we knew the past and present well enough, far fewer "surprises" would catch us unaware in the future. It pays to watch, and it especially pays to watch the largest systems—government, education, transportation, primary metals, finance, health care, energy—for they usually change very slowly and only after protracted debate and consensus building.

No one should have any difficulty with the notion that many of the developments causing turmoil and confusion in each of these systems today were being widely discussed—even passionately advocated or resisted—at least 10 or more years ago. Five or 10 years from now no one should find it hard to look back to today and discover that the same was true.

Administrators in large institutions know that very long lead times are often required before major decisions can be initiated and fully implemented. They also know that the environment can change in peculiar, sometimes unpredictable ways while these decisions are coursing through the system. The result can be that by the time the decisions should have been fully implemented, the world will have changed so much that they must be abandoned or radically altered. To the extent, however, that the original expectations were shattered by forces arising from large systems, why should administrators be surprised by the outcome? They may be exceedingly disappointed that they have persevered in a losing battle, but they should not be surprised.

Real surprises usually come from failing to keep track of small-scale developments in the external environment, not from excluding small-scale developments within one's own system. By systematically following these external developments it is possible not only to anticipate the directions and potential impacts of the slower, more pronounced, more profoundly influential changes but also to obtain the early warning needed for timely adjustments of strategy. Emerging patterns of events, the ebb and flow of particular sets of issues that can be revealed by close monitoring, provide a basis for forecasts relevant to policy. These forecasts are intuitive, to be sure, and perhaps seen only dimly in outline, but they are nonetheless the best forecasts available.

Even when the output from scanning consists of forecasts, we must still make our own judgments about the future, because we must decide what is relevant and we must make judgments as to whether we agree with the given forecasts. The same process is at play when we read newspapers, journals, reports, and government documents or listen to a broadcast. We constantly make personal forecasts on the basis of sparse and fragmented historical data in an attempt to distill the future that may be implied.

This process of trying to infer the future by mentally extending current or historical data is sometimes called "implicit forecasting." Such forecasting is obviously as useful as it is unavoidable when it comes to obtaining an

*It pays to watch . . . the largest systems . . . for they usually change very slowly.*

appreciation of the broad outlines of possible futures. By itself, however, implicit forecasting is not sufficient when it comes to making today's decisions about our own most important long-range issues—the direction of a career, the development of a profession, the survival of an institution, department, or program, for example. In such cases, the need is also for methods that deal much more formally, systematically, and comprehensively with the nature and likely dynamics of future events, trends, and policy choices.

It is easy to see why our implicit forecasts of the general context are progressively less trustworthy as the questions at stake become more important. These forecasts are entirely subjective, they are no doubt idiosyncratic, they are often made on topics we are unqualified to assess because of a lack of relevant experience or knowledge, they rest very largely on unspoken arguments from historical precedent or analogy, and they are haphazard in that they are made primarily in response to information we receive that is itself usually developed haphazardly or opportunistically.

As futures research has developed since the mid-1960s, much work has gone into the invention and application of techniques intended to overcome these and other limitations of widely practiced methods of forecasting. In general, the newer methods are alike in that they tend to deal as explicitly and systematically as possible with the various elements of alternative futures, the aim being to provide the wherewithal for users to retrace the steps taken. The following paragraphs highlight some of these methods.

### Genius forecasting
Apart from implicit forecasting, the most common approach to forecasting throughout history has been for a single individual simply to make explicit guesstimates about the future. In their weaker moments, many bright and otherwise well-informed people—including even futures researchers—are sometimes cajoled into offering such guesstimates, which typically take the form of one-line forecasts ("cancer will be cured," "no ship will ever be sunk by a bomb," or "the end is near"). But if they are persuaded to reflect on the future in a widely ranging way, to try to articulate the underlying logic of affairs and its

likely evolution over time, to reason through the obvious alternatives and imagine the not so obvious ones, when in short they offer a careful but creative image of the future in its richness and complexity, then a much different process is involved. It has no common name, but in futures research it is often lightly called "genius forecasting." It is a powerful and highly cost-effective way to obtain forecasts if the "genius" is indeed thoughtful, imaginative, and well read in many areas.

The disadvantages of genius forecasting are clear enough to require no enumeration here. "In the end, genius forecasting depends on more than the genius of the forecaster; it depends on luck and insight. There may be many geniuses whose forecasts are made with full measure of both, but it is nearly impossible to recognize them *a priori,* and this, of course, is the weakness of the method" (Gordon 1972, p. 167).

If used properly, however, the strengths of the method usually outweigh its weaknesses. The probability of the integrated forecast produced by the "genius" is certain to be virtually zero. Time will show that the forecast was oversimplified, led astray by biases, and ignorant of critical possibilities. Yet the genius has the ability to identify unprecedented future events, to imagine current policies that might be abandoned, to assess the interplay of trends and future events in a far more meaningful way than any existing model can, to trace out the significance of this interplay, to identify opportunities for action that no one else might ever see, and to explain assumptions and reasoning. Although the genius forecast will be both "wrong" and incomplete, it will nevertheless have provided something very useful: an *intelligent* base case.

Occasionally, genius forecasts can serve as the only forecasts in a study. This approach makes excellent sense in studies being accomplished under severely constrained time and resources. Increasingly in futures research, however, studies are *begun* by commissioning one or more genius forecasts, which take the form of essays or scenarios of one sort or another. With them in hand, the investigators explore them carefully for omissions and inconsistencies, and then the forecasts are carefully pulled apart to identify the specific trends, events, and policies that appear to warrant detailed evaluation; that is, the most uncertain, problematical, intractable, and potentially valuable statements about the future can be selected. Being able to launch a more sophisticated forecasting effort from such a basis is much better than having random thoughts and blank paper.

### Extrapolation of mathematical trends

Most forecasters and some practitioners of futures research use techniques of mathematical trend extrapolation that are well understood, rest on a fairly adequate theoretical foundation, convey the impression of being scientific and objective, and in skilled hands are usually quick and inexpensive to use. One of the most commonly used techniques is regression analysis, one purpose of which is to estimate the predicted values of a trend (the dependent variable) from observed values of other trends (the independent variables). Hierarchical regression models are sometimes referred to as "causal" models if an observed statistical relationship exists between the independent and dependent variables, if the independent variables occur before the dependent variable, and if one can develop a reasonable explanation for the causal relationship. A forecast of the independent variables makes possible a forecast of the dependent ones to which they are statistically linked, whether the case is simple or complex. In either case, however, the purpose behind causal regression models is always to explain complex dynamic trends (for example, college and university enrollment patterns) in terms of elementary stable trends (for example, demographics or government spending).

When cause is not an essential factor, trends are often forecast using time as the independent variable. Much of the "trend extrapolation" in futures research takes this form. Common methods of time-series forecasting being used today are the smoothing, decomposition, and autoregression/moving average methods. Smoothing methods are used to eliminate randomness from a data series to identify an underlying pattern, if one exists, but they make no attempt to identify individual components of the underlying pattern. Decomposition methods can be used to identify those components—typically, the trend, the cycle, and the seasonal factors—which are then predicted individually. The recombination of these predicted patterns is the final forecast of the series. Like smoothing methods, decomposition methods lack a fully developed theoretical basis, but they are being used today because of their simplicity and short-term accuracy. Autoregression is essentially the same as the classical multivariate regression, the only difference being that the independent (predictor) variables are simply the time-lagged values of the dependent (predicted) variable. Because time-lagged values tend to be highly correlated, coupling autoregression with the moving average method produces a very general class of time-series models called autoregression/moving average (ARMA) models.

All regression and time-series methods rest on the assumption that the historical data can, by themselves, be used to forecast the future of a series. In other words, they assume that the future of a trend is exclusively a function of its past. This assumption, however, will always prove false eventually because of the influence of forces not measured by the time series itself. That is to say, unprecedented sorts of events always occur and affect the series, which is precisely why the historical data are so irregular.

These difficulties have not deterred many traditional analysts and long-range forecasters from using such methods and thereby generating dubious advice for their sponsors. Within futures research, however, these techniques—when used well—are applied in a very distinctive way. The objective is not to foretell the future, which is obviously impossible, but to provide purely extrapolative base-line projections to use as a point of reference when obtaining projections of the same trends by more appropriate methods. What would the world look like if past and current forces for change were allowed to play themselves out? What if nothing novel ever happened again? The only value of these mathematical forecasting techniques in futures research is to provide answers to these remarkably speculative questions. But once they are answered, a reference will have been established for getting on with more serious forecasting.

For example, in a study by Boucher and Neufeld (1981), a set of 111 trends was forecast 20 years hence both mathematically (using an ARMA technique) and judgmentally (using the Delphi technique). Analysis of the results showed that the average difference between the two sets of forecasts was over 15 percent. By the first forecasted year (which was less than a year from the date of the completion of the Delphi), the divergence already *averaged* more than 10 percent; by the 20th year, it had reached 20 percent. This result is interesting because even experienced managers usually accept mathematical forecasts uncritically. They like their apparent scientific objectivity, they have been trained in school to accept their plausibility, and acceptance has been reinforced by an endless stream of such projections from government, academia, and other organizations. Seeing judgmental and mathematical results side-by-side can thus be most instructive. Moreover, as some futures researchers believe, if the difference between such a pair of projections is 10 percent or more, it is probably worth examining in depth.

### The Delphi technique

Given the limitations of personal forecasting (implicit or genius) and of mathematical projections, it is now common—and usually wise—to rely on systematic methods for using a *group* of persons to prepare the forecasts and assessments needed in strategic planning. Experience suggests, however, that at least five conditions must be present before the decision to use a group should be made: (1) No "known" or "right" answers exist or can be had (that is, acceptable forecasts do not exist or are not available); (2) equally reputable persons disagree about the nature of the problem, the relative importance of various issues, and the probable future; (3) the questions to be investigated cross disciplinary, political, or jurisdictional lines, and no one individual is considered competent enough to cope with so many subjects; (4) cross-fertilization of ideas seems worthwhile and possible; and (5) a credible method exists for defining group consensus and evaluating group performance.

The fifth condition is especially important—and often slighted. As a matter of fact, the emphasis one places on this consideration often determines the method of group forecasting one chooses. If, for example, the person seeking the forecasts will be content with an oral summary of the results (or perhaps a memo for the record), then a conventional face-to-face meeting of some sort may be the appropriate method. If, at the other extreme, it is known that the intended user will insist on having a detailed comprehensive forecast and that the persons whose views should be solicited would never speak openly or calmly to each other at a face-to-face meeting, then a different scheme for eliciting, integrating, and reporting the forecasts would surely be required.

Considerations like these were responsible in large part for the invention of what is no doubt the most famous and popular of all forecasting methods associated with futures research: the Delphi technique. Delphi was designed to obtain consensus forecasts from a group of "experts" on the assumption that many heads are indeed often better than one, an assumption supported by the argument that a group estimate is at least as reliable as that of a randomly chosen expert (Dalkey 1969). But Delphi was developed to deal especially with the situation in which risks were inherent in bringing these experts together for a face-to-face meeting—for example, possible reluctance of some participants to revise previously expressed judgments, possible domination of the meeting by a powerful individual or clique, possible bandwagon effects on some issues, and similar problems of group psychology. The Delphi method was intended to overcome or minimize such obstacles to effective collaborative forecasting by four simple procedural rules, the first of which is desirable, the last three of which are mandatory.

*First, no participant is told the identity of the other members of the group,* which is easily accomplished if, as is common, the forecasts are obtained by means of questionnaires or individual interviews. When the Delphi is conducted in a workshop setting—one of the more productive ways to proceed in many cases—this rule cannot be honored, of course.

*Second, no single opinion, forecast, or other key input is attributed to the individual who provided it or to anyone else.* Delphi questionnaires, interviews, and computer conferences all easily provide this protection. In the workshop setting, it is more difficult to ensure, but it can usually be obtained by using secret ballots or various electronic machines that permit anonymous voting with immediate display of the distribution of answers from the group as a whole.

*Third, the results from the initial round of forecasting must be collated and summarized by an intermediary (the*

*experimenter), who feeds these data back to all partici-
pants and invites each to rethink his or her original answers in light of the responses from the group as a whole.*
If, for example, the participants have individually estimated an event's probability by some future year, the intermediary might compute the mean or median response,
the interquartile range or upper and lower envelopes of the
estimates, the standard deviation, and so forth, and pass
these data back to the panelists for their consideration in
making a new estimate. If the panelists provided qualitative information as well—for example, reasons for estimating the probabilities as they did or judgments as to the
consequences of the event if it were actually to occur—the
role of the intermediary would be to edit these statements,
eliminate the redundant ones, and arrange them in some
reasonable order before returning them for the group's
consideration.

*Fourth, the process of eliciting judgments and estimates*
(deriving the group response, feeding it back, and asking
for reestimates in light of the results obtained so far)
*should be continued until either of two things happens: The
consensus within the group is close enough for practical
purposes, or the reasons why such a consensus cannot be
achieved have been documented.*

In sum, the defining characteristics of Delphi are anonymity of the estimates, controlled feedback, and iteration.
The promise of Delphi was that if these characteristics
were preserved, consensus within the panel would sharpen
and the opinions or forecasts derived by the process would
be closer to the "true" answer than forecasts derived by
other judgmental approaches.

Thousands of Delphi studies of varying quality have
been conducted throughout the world since 1964, when the
first major report on the technique was published (Gordon
and Helmer 1964). The subjects forecast have ranged from
the future of absenteeism in the work force to the future of
war and along the way have included topics as diverse as
prospective educational technologies, the likely incidence
of breast cancer, the future of the rubber industry, the
design of an ideal telephone switchboard, and the future of
Delphi itself. Some of these studies proved to be extremely
helpful in strategic planning; a few virtually decided the
future of the sponsoring organization. But most had little

or no effect, apart from providing general background information or satisfying a momentary curiosity about this novel method of forecasting.

Part of the problem in many cases is that practitioners have had false hopes. The literature conveys the impression that Delphi is so powerful and simple that anyone can "run one" on any subject. What the literature often fails to mention is that no established conventions yet exist for any aspect of study design, execution, analysis, or reporting. Intermediaries, who are the key to useful and responsible results, are very much on their own. As novices they should examine studies by others, but because these studies are all different, it may be very difficult to find or recognize good models. Even with an excellent model in hand, the newcomer cannot fully appreciate what it means to use it. Only through practice can one discover the significance of four key facts about Delphi: (1) The amount of information and data garnered through the process can and will explode from round to round; (2) good questions are difficult to devise, and the better the design of the questions asked, the more likely it is that good participants will resign from the panel out of what has been called the BIF factor—boredom, irritation, and fatigue—because they will be asked to answer the same challenging questions again and again for each trend or event in the set they are forecasting; (3) the likelihood of such attrition within the panel means not that the questions should be cheapened but that large panels must be established so that each participant will have fewer questions to answer, which is very time consuming; (4) Delphi itself does not include procedures for synthesizing the entire set of specific forecasts and supporting arguments it produces, so that when the study is "completed," the work has usually just begun. And if, as one hopes, the intermediary and the panelists take the process and the questions seriously, the probability is high that the schedule will slip, the budget will be overrun, and so on and on.

Another reason that success with Delphi is hard to achieve is that, despite 20 years of serious applications, very little is known about how and why the consensus-building process in Delphi works or what it actually produces. No wide-ranging research on the fundamentals of the method has been done for more than a decade. According to Olaf Helmer, one of the inventors of Delphi, "Delphi still lacks a completely sound theoretical basis. . . . Delphi experience derives almost wholly either from studies carried out without proper experimental controls or from controlled experiments in which students are used as surrogate experts" (Linstone and Turoff 1975, p. v). The same is true today. The practical implication is that most of what is "known" about Delphi consists of rules of thumb based on the experience of individual practitioners.

For example, a goal of Delphi is to facilitate a sharpening of consensus forecasts from round to round of interrogation. And, in fact, there probably has yet to be a Delphi study in which the consensus among the participating experts did not actually grow closer on almost all of the estimates requested (as measured by, say, a decline in the size of the interquartile range of estimates). Yet the limited empirical evidence available on this phenomenon is replete with suggestions that increased consensus is produced only in slight part by the panelists' deliberations on the group feedback from the earlier round. The greater part of the shift seems to come from two other causes: (1) The panelists simply reread the questions and understood them better, and (2) the panelists are biased by the group's response in the preceding round of interrogation (that is, they allow themselves to drift toward the mean or median answer). The difficulty posed by this situation—which is far from atypical of the problems presented by Delphi—is that no way has yet been found to sort out the effects of these different influences on the final forecast. Accordingly, the investigator must be extremely careful when interpreting the results. Claims that Delphi is "working" are always suspect.

On the positive side, though again as a strictly practical, nontheoretical matter, Delphi appears to have a number of important advantages as a group evaluation or forecasting technique. It is not difficult to explain the essence of the method to potential participants or to one's superiors. It is quite likely that some types of forecasts could not be obtained from a group without the guarantee of anonymity and the opportunity for second thoughts in later rounds (certainly true when hostile stake holders are jointly evaluating the implications of policy actions that might affect them differently). Areas of agreement and disagreement within the panel can be readily identified, thanks to the straightforward presentation of data. Perhaps most important, every participant's opinion can be heard on the forecasts in every round, and every participant has the opportunity to comment on every qualitative argument or assessment. For this reason, it becomes much easier to determine the uncertainties that responsible persons have about the problem under study. If the panelists are chosen carefully, a full spectrum of hopes, fears, and other expectations can be defined.

When successes with Delphi occur, it would seem that the explanation is not that the panel converged from round to round (which, as indicated earlier, almost always happens). Nor is it that the mean or median response moved toward the "true" answer (which is something that no one could know at the time). Rather, it is that the investigation was conducted professionally and that the results did in fact have the effect of increasing the user's understanding of the uncertainties surrounding the problem, the range of strategic options available in light of those uncertainties, and the need to monitor closely the possible, real-world consequences of options that may actually be implemented.

Delphi has been used in many policy studies in higher education. In one case, it was used to determine priorities for a program in family studies (Young 1978). Nash (1978), after reviewing its use in a number of studies concerning educational goals and objectives, curriculum and campus planning, and effectiveness and cost-benefit measures, concluded that the Delphi is a convenient methodology appropriate for a non-research-oriented population. The technique has also been used in a number of planning studies (Judd 1972). For example, it was used as a tool for getting planning data to meet the needs of adult part-time students in North Carolina (Fendt 1978).

In general, the more successful practitioners of Delphi appear to have tried to follow the 15 steps presented in figure 8. These "rules" may appear platitudinous, and virtually no one has ever followed all of them in a single Delphi. Yet the intrinsic quality and practical value of Delphi results are certain to be a function of the degree to which they are followed.

*Every participant's opinion can be heard on the forecasts in every round, and every participant has the opportunity to comment.*

**FIGURE 8**
**STEPS IN A PERFECT DELPHI**

1. Understand Delphi (for example, that at least two rounds of interrogation are necessary).

2. Specify the subject and the objectives. (Don't study "the future." Study alternative futures of X—and do so with clear purpose.)

3. Specify whether the forecasting mode to be adopted is exploratory or normative—or some clear combination of both.

4. Specify all desired products, level of effort, responsibilities, and schedule.

5. Specify the uses to which the results will be put, if they are actually achieved.

6. Exploit the methodology and substantive results developed in earlier Delphi studies.

7. Design the study so that it includes only judgmental questions (except in extreme cases), and see to it that these questions are precisely phrased and cover all topics of interest as specifically as possible.

8. Design all rounds of the study before administering the first

### Other group techniques

Delphi is generally considered one of the better techniques of pooling the insight, experience, imagination, and judgment of those who are knowledgeable in strategic matters and who have an obligation to deal with them responsibly. Many other ways, however, can be used to exploit the power of groups in forecasting and futures research: brainstorming, gaming, synectics, the nominal group technique, focus groups, and others, including the Quick Environmental Scanning Technique (QUEST), the Focused Planning Effort (FPE), and the Delphi Decision Support System ($D_2S_2$™). The last three are discussed in this section because they are currently used in futures research.

round. (Don't forget that this step includes the design of forms or software for collating the responses.)

9. Design the survey instrument so that the questions are explained clearly and simply, can be answered as painlessly as possible, and can be answered responsibly.

10. Include appropriate historical data and a set of assumptions about the future in the survey instrument so that the respondents will all be dealing with future developments in the context of the same explicit past and "given" future.

11. Assemble a group of respondents capable of answering the questions creatively, in depth, and on schedule, and large enough to ensure that all important points of view are represented.

12. Collate the responses wisely, consistently, and promptly.

13. Analyze the data wisely, consistently, and promptly.

14. Probe the methodology and the substantive results constantly during and after the effort to identify problems and important needed improvements.

15. Synthesize and present the final results to management intelligently.

QUEST (Nanus 1982) was developed to quickly and inexpensively provide the grist for strategic planning: forecasts of events and trends, an indication of the interrelationships among them and hence the opportunities for policy intervention, and scenarios that synthesize these results into coherent alternative futures. It is a face-to-face technique, accomplished through two day-long meetings spaced about a month apart. The procedure produces a comprehensive analysis of the external environment and an assessment of an organization's strategic options.

A QUEST exercise usually begins with the recognition of a potentially critical strategic problem. The process requires a moderator, who may be an outside consultant, to facilitate posing questions that challenge obsolete management positions and to maintain an objective perspective on ideas generated during the activity. The process also requires a project coordinator, who must be an "insider," to facilitate translating the results of QUEST exercises into scenarios that address strategic questions embedded in the organizational culture.

QUEST involves four steps. The first step, preparation, requires defining the strategic issue to be analyzed, selecting participants (12 to 15), developing an information notebook elaborating the issue, and selecting distraction-free workshop sites.

The second step is to conduct the first planning session. It is important that at least one day be scheduled to provide sufficient time to discuss the strategic environment in the broadest possible terms. This discussion includes identifying the organization's strategic mission, the objectives reflected in this mission, key stake holders, priorities, and critical environmental events and trends that may have significant impacts on the organization. Much of this time will be spent evaluating the magnitude and likelihood of these impacts and their cross-impacts on each other and on the organization's strategic posture. Participants are encouraged to focus on strategic changes but not on the strategic implications of these changes. This constraint is imposed to delay evaluations and responses until a complete slate of alternatives is developed.

The third step is to summarize the results of the first planning session in two parts: (1) a statement of the organization's strategic position, mission, objectives, stake holders, and so on, and (2) a statement of alternative scenarios illustrating possible external environments facing the organization over the strategic period. It is important that the report be attributed to the group, not sections to particular individuals. Correspondingly, it is important that the report reflect that ideas were considered on the basis of merit, not who advanced them. The report should be distributed a few days before the second group meeting, the final step.

The second meeting focuses on the report and the strategic options facing the organization. These options are evaluated for their responsiveness to the changing external environment and for their consistency with internal strengths and weaknesses. While this process will not produce an immediate change in strategy, it should result in directions to evaluate the most important options in greater depth. Consequently, a QUEST exercise ends with specific assignments vis-à-vis the general nature of the inquiry needed to evaluate each option, including a completion date.

The Focused Planning Effort was developed in 1971 (Boucher 1972). Like QUEST, it is an unusual kind of face-to-face meeting that draws systematically on the judgment and imagination of line and staff managers to define future threats and opportunities and find practical actions for dealing with them. Because the process is perfectly general—that is, it can be used to address *any* complex judgmental questions on future mission or strategic policy—the range of applications has been widely varied. In recent years, topics have ranged from the potential merit of technologies to improve agricultural yields, to alternative futures for the data communications industry, to the assessment of human resources in the future.

The FPE has the following features, which in concert make it a distinctive approach to strategic forecasting and policy assessment:

- All topics relevant to the subject chosen for investigation are explored, one by one and in context with each other. An FPE seeks to be comprehensive. Typically, the participants define the organization's mission, objectives, and goals, and then identify, forecast, and evaluate several issues: (1) the elements of their business environment, including relevant prospective social, economic, technological, and political developments; (2) the alternatives open to the organization; (3) criteria for deciding among the alternatives vis-à-vis the organization's mission, objectives, and goals; (4) the degree to which each important alternative satisfies the criteria; and (5) the dynamic cross-support interrelationships among the preferred alternatives.
- No idea is off-limits. As in brainstorming, the first objective is to expand the group's sense of the options available.
- All participants have a full and equal opportunity to influence the outcome at each step. In particular, each

participant evaluates every important issue raised after it has been examined in face-to-face discussion by the group.

- These individual evaluations become the group's response, but the range of opinion (that is, the uncertainty or lack of consensus) is captured and serves as a basis for clarifying differences and sharpening the group's final judgment.
- Thus, the participants typically respond to the opinion of the group, not to the opinions of individuals within the group. In this way, team building is enhanced and personal confrontations avoided.
- The FPE is highly systematic, thanks to the use of an interlocking combination of methods that have proven successful in structuring and eliciting judgment. Unlike QUEST, which uses a fixed combination of techniques, the mix used in an FPE varies depending on the subject, the number of participants, and the time available. It can include relevance tree analysis, brainstorming, the Delphi technique, subjective trend extrapolation, polling, operational gaming, cross-support and cross-impact analysis, and scenario development. And while such techniques are used in the FPE, they are not given a particular prominence; they are treated as means, not ends.
- All judgments on important issues are quantified through individual votes, usually taken on private ballots. This quantification permits objective comparisons of the subjective inputs. Anonymous voting enables everyone to speak his mind.
- The judgment of the group as a whole is available to each participant at the completion of every step of the FPE. These results then become the basis of the next step, thus helping to ensure that each part of the problem being addressed is dealt with in a context.
- The major results of the FPE are available at the end of the activity, in writing, and each participant has a copy of the results to take with him.

The FPE process has three parts. The first—premeeting design—is the key. Each FPE requires its own design, and the process does not involve a pat formula. The design phase usually requires 10 to 15 days, spread over a few calendar weeks. During this phase, the problem is structured, needed historical data are collected, the FPE logic is defined in detail, and first-cut answers to the more important questions are obtained through interviews or a questionnaire or both. These preliminary answers serve as a check on the FPE design and as a basis for the discussion that will occur during the FPE itself. Ordinarily, this information is gathered from a larger group of people than the one that will participate in the FPE.

The final design is usually formulated in two ways: first, as an agenda, which is distributed to the participants, and, second, as a set of written "modules," each describing a specific task to be completed in the FPE, its purpose, the methods to be used, the anticipated outcomes, and the time allotted for each step in the task. These modules serve as the basis of the sign-off in the final pre-FPE review.

The second part of the process is the FPE itself. The number of participants can range from as few as seven or eight to as many as 20 to 25. The FPE normally requires two to three full days of intensive work, though FPEs have run anywhere from one to 12 days. The period can be consecutive or be spread out in four-hour blocks over a schedule that is convenient to all participants. Typically, the FPE is preceded by a luncheon or dinner meeting and a brief roundtable discussion, which serves to break the ice and helps to clarify expectations about the work to follow.

The FPE can be manual or computer-assisted. $D_2S_2$™, developed by the Policy Analysis Company, uses a standard floppy disk and personal computer, usually connected to a large-screen monitor or projector (Renfro 1985). The larger the group of participants, the greater the desirability of using such computer assistance. Not only is the collation of individual votes greatly speeded; in addition, the software developed by some consulting organizations that provide the FPE service (for example, the ICS Group and the Policy Analysis Company) can reveal the basis of differences among subgroups of the participants and draw certain inferences that are implied by the data but not readily apparent on the basis of the estimates themselves. In $D_2S_2$™, it includes confidence weighting, vote sharing, and vote assignment.

Although the design of the FPE is quite detailed, it is never rigid. On-the-spot changes are always required during the FPE in light of the flow of the group's discussion and the discoveries it makes. But the design makes it possible to know the opportunity costs of these adjustments and hence when it is appropriate to rein in the group and return to the agenda.

The final part of the process is postmeeting analysis and documentation of the results and specification of areas requiring action or further analysis. Although the principal findings will be known at the end of the FPE, this postmeeting activity is important because the results will have been quantified, and it is necessary to transcend the numbers and capture in words the reasons for various estimates, the basis of irreducible disagreements, and the areas of greatest uncertainty. Additionally, it may be necessary to perform special analyses to distill the full implications of these results.

### Cross-impact analysis

Cross-impact analysis is an advanced form of forecasting that builds upon the results achieved through the various subjective and objective methods described in the preceding pages. Although as many as 16 distinct types of cross-impact analysis models have been identified (Linstone 1983), an idea common to each is that separate and explicit account is taken of the causal connections among a set of forecasted developments (perhaps derived by genius forecasting or Delphi). Among some futures researchers, a model that includes only the interactions of events is called a cross-impact model. A model that includes only the interactions of events on forecasted trends but not the impacts of the events on each other is called a "trend impact analysis" (TIA) model. In the general case, however, "cross-impact analysis" is increasingly coming to refer to models in which event-to-event and event-to-trend impacts are considered simultaneously. Constructing such a model involves estimating how the occurrence of each event in the set might affect ("impact") the probability of occurrence of every other event in the set as well as the nominal forecast of each of the trends. (These nominal trend forecasts may be derived through mathematical trend extrapolation or subjective projections.) When these relationships have been specified, it then becomes possible to let events "happen"—either randomly in accordance with their estimated probability or in some prearranged way—and then trace out a distinct, plausible, and internally consistent future. Importantly, it also becomes possible to introduce policy choices into the model to explore their potential value.

Development of a cross-impact model and defining the cross-impact relationships is tedious and demanding. The most complex model that can be built today (using existing software) can include as many as 100 events and 85 trends. Although they may seem like small numbers—after all, how many truly important problems can be described with reference to only 85 trends and 100 possible "surprise" events?—consider the magnitude of the effort required to specify such a model. First, it is necessary to identify where "hits" exist among pairs of events or event-trend pairs. For a model of this size, 18,400 possible cross-impact relationships need to be evaluated (9,900 for the events on the events and 8,500 for the events on the trends). This evaluation is done judgmentally, usually by a team of experts. Experience suggests that hits will be found in about 20 percent of the possible cases, which means that some 3,700 impacts of events on events or events on trends will need to be described in detail.

How are they described? In the most sophisticated model, seven estimates are required to depict the connection between an event impacting on the probability of another event:

1. Length of time from the occurrence of the impact*ing* event before its effects would be felt first by the impact*ed* event;
2. The degree of change in the probability of the impacted event at that point when the impacting event would have its maximum impact;
3. The length of time from the occurrence of the impacting event until this maximum impact (that is, change in probability) would be achieved;
4. The length of time from the occurrence of the impacting event that this maximum impact level would endure;
5. If the maximum impact might taper off, the change in probability of the impacted event when its new, stable level were reached;

6. The length of time from the occurrence of the impacting event to reach this stable impact level;

7. A judgment as to whether or not these effects had been taken into account when estimating the probability of the impacting and impacted events in the Delphi.

Eight cross-impact factors need to be estimated to describe the hit of an event on a trend. The first seven are the same as those specified above, except that estimates 2 and 5 are not for changes in probability but for changes in the nominal forecasted value of the trend. The eighth estimate specifies whether the changes in the trend values are to be multiplicative or additive.

In short, if we have 3,700 hits to describe and if, say, 60 percent of them (2,220) are impacts of events on events and 40 percent (1,480) are of events on trends, then 27,380 judgments must be made to construct the model (that is, 2,220 × 7 + 1,480 × 8). With these estimates, plus the initial forecasts of the probability of the events and the level of the trends, the model is complete. It can then be run to generate an essentially unlimited number of individual futures. In one version of cross-impact analysis, developed at the University of Southern California, the model can be run so that the human analyst has the opportunity to intervene in the future as it emerges, introducing policies that can change the probabilities of the events or the level of the trends. This model operates as follows:

1. The time period is divided into annual intervals.
2. The cross-impact model computes the probabilities of occurrences of each of the events in the first year.
3. A random number generator is used to decide which (if any) of the events occurred in the first year. (It should perhaps be emphasized that once the estimated probability of an event exceeds zero, the event *can* happen. No one may think it *will* happen, or conversely everyone may be convinced that it will. If it happens—or fails to happen—the event is a surprise. In cross-impact analysis, events are made to "happen" in accordance with their probability; that is, a 10 percent event will happen in 10 percent of all futures, a 90 percent event will happen in 90 percent of

them, and so on. One would be surprised indeed if he or she were betting on a future world in which the 10 percent event was expected not to happen but did, and the 90 percent event was expected to happen but did not.)

4. The results of the simulated first year are used to adjust the probabilities of the remaining events in subsequent years and the trend forecasts for the end of the first year and their projected performance for the subsequent years.

5. The computer reports these results to the human analysts interacting with the simulation and stops, awaiting additional instructions.

6. The human analysts assume that the simulated time is real time and assess the result as they think they would had this outcome actually taken place. They decide which aspects of their strategy (if any) they would change and input these changes to the computer model, which then simulates the next year's results using the same procedure described for the first year.

7. The simulation repeats these steps until all of the years in the strategic time period have been decided (Enzer 1983, p. 80).

When all intervals are complete, one possible long-term future is described by modified trend projections over time, the events that occurred and the years in which they occurred, a list of the policy changes introduced by the analysts, and the impacts of those policy changes on the resulting scenario. The analysts may also prepare a narrative describing how they viewed the simulated conditions and how effective their policy choices appeared in retrospect.

By repeating the simulation many times, perhaps with different groups of analysts, it is possible to develop a number of alternative futures, thereby minimizing surprise when the transition is made from the analytic model to the real world. Perhaps the most important contribution that the USC model (or cross-impact methods generally) can make in improving strategic planning, however, is in its continued use as the strategic plan is implemented (Enzer 1980a, 1980b). The uncertainty captured in the initial model will be subject to change as anticipations give way to reality. Such changes may in turn suggest revisions to the plan.

Models of such complexity are expensive to develop and currently can be run only on a large, mainframe computer. For these reasons, their use is warranted only in the most seriously perplexing and vital situations. A number of less complex microcomputer-based cross-impact models are under development, however. For example, the Institute for Future Systems Research, Inc. (Greenwood, South Carolina), has developed a cross-impact model that can be run on an Apple IIe. Although in the alpha stage of development, this model has the capability of 30 events and 20 policies impacting three trends.

Much simpler models are commonplace. In essence, they are the same, but the rigorous calculations required for complex models can be approximated manually while preserving much of the qualitative value of the results, such as identifying the most important events in a small set. In the simplified manual calculation, the impact of the event is multiplied times its probability: A 50 percent probable event will have 50 percent of its impact occur, a 75 percent event will have 75 percent of its impact occur, and so on. This impact probability is calculated and added or subtracted, depending on its direction, to the level of the extrapolated trend at point $a$ (see figure 9). The event-impacted forecast for the years from $b$ are determined by connecting points $b$ and $a$ with the dashed line as shown. This process is repeated for each of the potential surprise events until a final expected value of the event-impacted indicator is developed. The event with the highest product of probability and impact is the most important event or the event having the greatest potential impact on the trend. This simple calculation is the basis of cross-impact analysis, though the detail and complexity (not to mention effort and cost) can be much greater in computer simulations.[1]

*Policy impact analysis*
Most of the techniques of futures research developed in the last 20 years provide information about futures in which the decision makers who have the information are pre-

[1]For a more detailed discussion of this approach, including an example from the field of education, see Renfro and Morrison 1982.

## FIGURE 9
## QUALITATIVE EXAMPLE OF AN EVENT-IMPACTED INDICATOR

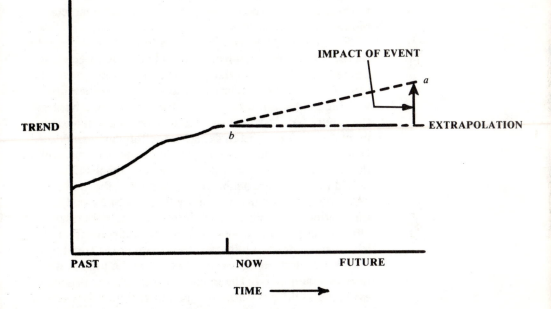

Source: Renfro and Morrison 1982.

sumed not to use it; that is, new decisions and policies are not included in the futures described by these techniques (Renfro 1980c). The very purpose of this information, however, is to guide decision makers as they adopt policies designed to achieve more desirable futures—to change their expected future. In this sense, traditional techniques of futures research describe futures that happen *to* the decision makers, but decision makers use this information to work toward futures that happen *for* them. Apart from policy-oriented uses of cross-impact analysis, policy impact analysis is the first model that focuses on identifying and evaluating policies, strategies, and decisions designed to respond to information generated by traditional techniques of futures research.

The steps involved in policy impact analysis are based on the results obtained from the probabilistic forecasting procedure outlined previously. When the events have been ranked according to their importance (their probability-weighted impacts), these results are typically fed back to the group, panel, or decision makers providing the judgmental estimates used to generate the forecast. As this group was asked to select and evaluate the surprise events, they are now asked to nominate specific policies that would modify the probability and impact of those events. Decision makers may change the forecast of a trend in three principal ways: first, by implementing policies to change the probability of one or more of the events that have been judged to influence the future of the trend; second, by implementing policies to change the timing, direction, or magnitude of the impact of one or more of the events; and third, by adopting policies that in effect create new events. If all or most of the important events affecting a trend have been considered, then new events should have little or no direct impact on the indicator. For some events, such as the return of double-digit inflation, it may not be possible for the decision makers at one university to change the events' probability, but it may be possible to affect the timing and magnitude of their impacts if they did occur. For example, it may not be possible to affect the president's decision to issue a particular executive order, such as cutting federal aid to higher education, but its impact can be diminished if administrators develop other sources of funding. Usually it is possible to identify policies that change both the probability and the impact of each event (Renfro 1980a).

Policies are typically nominated on the basis of their effect on one particular event. To ensure that primary (or secondary) impacts on other events do not upset the intended effect of the policy, the potential impact of each policy on all events should be reviewed, easily done by the use of a simple chart like the one shown in figure 10.

Policies can impact the forecasts of an indicator in three ways: through the events, through the events and directly on the trends, and directly on the trends only. The relationship of policies to trends to the indicators might be envisioned as shown in figure 11. The policies that affect the indicator through events have four avenues of impact. A policy can change the probability of an event by making it more or less likely to occur, or a policy can change the impact of an event by increasing or changing the level of an impact, changing the timing of an impact, or changing both level and timing of an impact (see figure 12).[2]

The new estimates of probability and impact are used to recalculate the probabilistic forecasts along the lines outlined earlier. The difference between the probabilistic forecast and the policy-impacted forecast shows the benefit of implementing each of the policies identified. Completed output of all of the steps results in three forecasts: the extrapolated surprise-free forecast, the probabilistic event-impacted forecast, and the policy-impacted forecast.

To illustrate, suppose that the policy issue being studied is enrollment in liberal arts baccalaureate programs and that measurements of those enrollments since 1945 are part of the data base available to a research study team. Further assume that those enrollments were forecast to decrease over the next 10 years, although the desired future would be one in which they would remain the same or increase. In this stage of the model, the team would first identify those events that could affect enrollments

*A policy can change the probability of an event by making it more or less likely to occur.*

---

[2]If a computer-based routine is used in policy impact analysis, numerical estimates must be developed to describe completely the shape and timing of the impacts, which, for the impact of one event on a trend, may require as many as eight estimates. These detailed mathematical estimates quickly mushroom into a monumental task that can overwhelm the patience and intellectual capacities of the most dedicated professionals if the task is not structured and managed to ease the burden. For a discussion of the details of the numerical estimates, see Renfro 1980b.

## FIGURE 10
## POLICIES-TO-EVENTS MATRIX

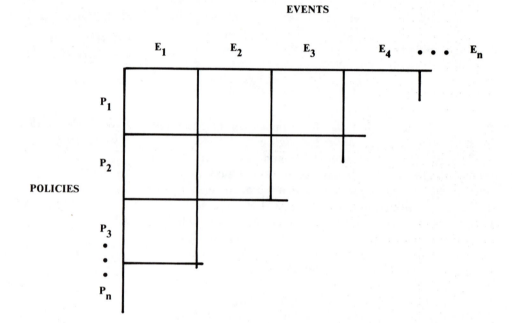

EVENTS

$E_1$     $E_2$     $E_3$     $E_4$  • • •  $E_n$

POLICIES

$P_1$

$P_2$

$P_3$
•
•
•
$P_n$

Source: Renfro 1980b.

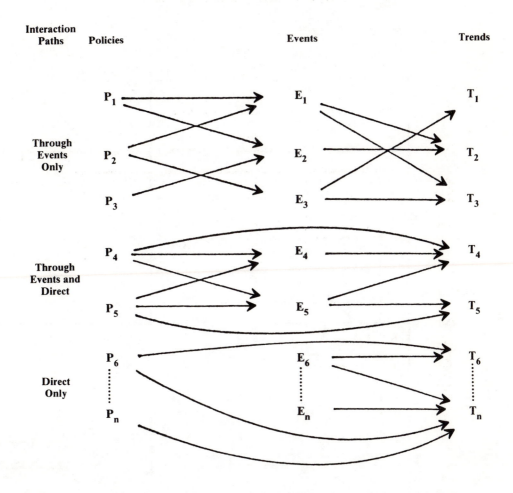

**FIGURE 11**
**RELATIONSHIP OF POLICIES TO EVENTS TO TRENDS:**
**THREE WAYS POLICIES IMPACT TRENDS**

Source: Renfro 1980b.

adversely—for example, a sudden jump in the rate of inflation, sharply curtailed federally funded financial aid, a
significant cut in private financial support, and so on. The
team would also identify events that could positively affect
enrollments—for example, commercial introduction of low-

# FIGURE 12
# IMPACT OF POLICY CHANGES

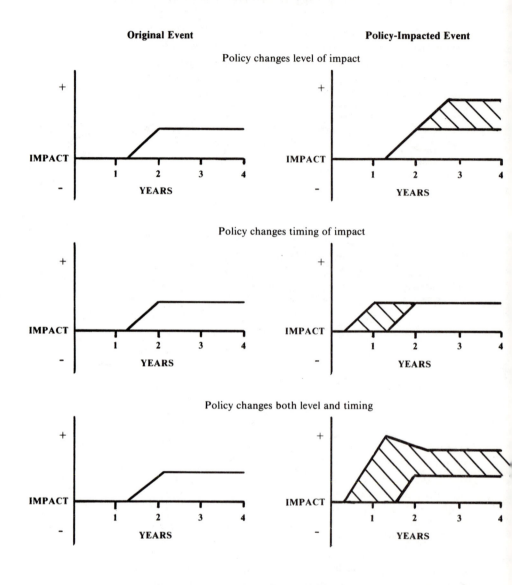

Source: Renfro 1980b.

cost, highly sophisticated CAI programs for use on home personal computers for mid-career retraining, a new government program to help fund the efforts of major corporations to provide continuing professional education programs for their employees, and so on. Such events may positively affect enrollments because a widely held assumption of liberal arts education is that it facilitates the development of thinking and communication skills easily translatable to a wide variety of requirements for occupational skills.

The next step would be to identify possible policies that could affect those events (or that could affect enrollments directly). For example, policies could be designed to increase enrollments by aggressively pursuing marketing strategies lauding the value of a liberal arts education as essential preparation for later occupational training. This strategy could be undertaken with secondary school counselors and students and with first- and second-year undergraduates and their advisors. Graduate and professional school faculty could be encouraged to consider adopting and publicly announcing admissions policies that grant preferential consideration to liberal arts graduates. Another policy could be to form coalitions with higher education organizations in other regions to press for increased federal aid to students and to institutions. With respect to the potential market in the business, industrial, and civil service sectors, policies with respect to establishing joint programs to provide liberal arts education on a part-time or "special" semester basis could be designed and implemented.

Policies could also be designed to maintain enrollments within the current student population. For example, one policy could concern an "early warning" system to identify liberal arts students who may be just experiencing academic difficulty. Others could be designed to inhibit attrition by improving the quality of the educational environment. Such policies would involve establishing faculty and instructional development programs and improving student personnel services, among others.

Next, the policies need to be linked formally to the events they are intended to affect, and their influence can then be evaluated. (As part of this process it is also important to look carefully at the cross-impacts among the policies themselves, as several of them may work against each other.) The result of this somewhat complex activity is a policy-impacted forecast for undergraduate baccalaureate programs, given the implementation of specific policies designed to improve enrollments. Thus, competing policy options may be evaluated by identifying those policies with the most favorable cost-benefit ratio, those having the most desirable effect, those with the most acceptable trade-offs, and so on.

Figure 13 is an example of a complete policy impact analysis where one may examine the relationship of an organizational goal for a particular trend, the extrapolative forecast, the probabilistic forecast, and the policy-impacted forecast. Note that the distinction between the projected forecasts is the result of the difference between the assumptions involved; that is, the extrapolative forecast does not include the probable impact of surprise events, whereas the probabilistic forecast does. Furthermore, the probabilistic forecast includes not only the effects of events on the trend but also the interactive effects of particular events on the trend. The policy impact forecast not only incorporates those features distinguishing probabilistic forecasts; it also includes estimates of the impact of policies on events affecting the trend as well as on the trend itself.

Evaluation occurs when the policy impact analysis model is iterated after the preferred policies have been implemented in the real world. That is, the process of monitoring begins anew, thereby enabling the staff to evaluate the effectiveness of the policies by comparing actual impacts with those forecast. Implementation of this model requires that a data base of social/educational indicators be updated and maintained by the scanning committee to evaluate the forecasts and policies and to add new trends as they are identified as being important in improving education in the future, that new and old events be reevaluated, and that probabilistic forecasts be updated to enable goals to be refined and reevaluated. This activity leads to the development of new policies or reevaluated old ones, which in turn enables the staff to update policy impacted forecasts (Morrison 1981b).[3]

[3]The techniques of futures research described here, particularly the probabilistic forecasting methods, have been developed only within the last 10

## FIGURE 13
## EXAMPLE OF A COMPLETE POLICY IMPACT ANALYSIS

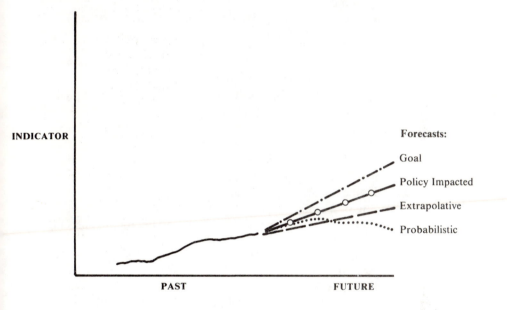

Source: Renfro 1980c.

to 20 years, and they have been used primarily in business and industry, with mixed results. The success of this model depends upon the ability of the staff to identify those events that may affect a trend directly or indirectly, accurately assign subjective probabilities to those events, design and obtain a reliable and valid data base of social/educational indicators, and specify appropriate factors that depict the interrelationships among the events, the trends, and the policies. The efficacy of the policy impact analysis model depends upon the close interaction of the research staff and decision makers within each stage of the model.

### The scenario

A key tool of integrative forecasting is the scenario—a story about the future. Many types of scenarios exist (Boucher 1984), but in general they are written as a history of the future describing developments across a period ranging from a few years to a century or more or as a slice of time at some point in the future. The scenarios as future history are a more useful tool in planning because they explain the developments along the way that lead to the particular circumstances found in the final state in the future.

A good scenario has a number of properties. To be useful in planning, it should be credible, it should be self-contained (in that it includes the important developments central to the issue being addressed), it should be internally consistent, it should be consistent with one's impression of how the world really works, it should clearly identify the events that are pivotal in shaping the future described, and it should be interesting and readable to ensure its use. Scenarios have been used both as launching devices to stimulate thinking about the future at the beginning of a study and as wrap-ups designed to summarize, integrate, and communicate the many detailed results of a forecasting study. For example, the information generated in the policy impact analysis process can easily be used to generate scenarios. A random number generator is used to determine which events happen and when. This sequence of events provides the outline of a scenario. With this technique, a wide range of scenarios can quickly be produced.

Frequently, several alternative scenarios are written, each based upon a central theme. For example, in the 1970s many studies on energy resources focused on three scenarios: (1) an energy-rich scenario, in which continued technological innovations and increased energy production eliminate energy shortages; (2) a muddling-through scenario, in which events remain essentially out of control and no resolution of the energy situation is realized; and (3) an energy-scarce scenario, in which we are unable to increase production or to achieve desired levels of conservation.

By creating multiple scenarios, one hopes to gain further insight into not only the potential range of demographic, technological, political, social, and economic trends and events but also how these developments may interact with each other, given various chance events and policy initiatives. Each scenario deals with a particular sequence of developments. Of course, if the scenarios are based on the results from earlier forecasting, the range of possibilities should already be reasonably well known, and the scenarios will serve to synthesize this knowledge. If, however, the earlier research has not been done, then the scenarios must be made of whole cloth. This practice is very common; indeed, some consulting organizations recommend it. Such scenarios can be quite effective, as long as the user recognizes that the product is actually a form of genius forecasting and shares all of the strengths and weaknesses of that approach.

Slice-of-time scenarios serve to provide a context for planning; indeed, they are similar to the budgeting or enrollment assumptions that often accompany planning instructions. Yet instead of single assumptions for each planning parameter, a range of assumptions may be considered. In turn, assumptions for different parameters are woven together to form internally consistent wholes, each of which forms a particular scenario, and the set may then be distributed as background for a new cycle of planning.

Multiple scenarios communicate to planners that while the future is unknowable, it may be anticipated and its possible forms can surely be better understood. In the language of strategic planning, a plan may be assessed against any scenario to test its "robustness." An effective plan, therefore, is one that recognizes the possibility of any plausible scenario. For example, in a planning conference with the president, the academic vice president might speculate how a particular strategy being proposed would "play itself out" if the future generally followed Scenario I and, then, what would happen given Scenario II. Heydinger has developed several plausible scenarios for higher education, which, although lacking the specificity required for actual institutional planning purposes, convey the flavor of a scenario (see figure 14).

The analysis of multiple scenarios requires attention to a number of factors discussed elsewhere in this monograph—improbable yet important developments (Heydinger and Zentner 1983). Moreover, in developing the scenarios, it is helpful to recognize that they can be used to describe futures on almost any level of generality, from higher education on the national level to the outlook for an individual

## FIGURE 14
## POSSIBLE SCENARIOS FOR HIGHER EDUCATION

### 1. The Official Future

Enrollments are down, and while adult and part-time students are more numerous, their presence has not offset the decline of traditional-age students. One in 10 state colleges has closed in the last seven years, and 25 percent of liberal arts colleges have closed since 1980. With the supply of traditional college-age students resurging, however, a mood of optimism is returning to campuses.

Industry establishes its own training facilities at an unheard-of pace and competes with higher education for the best postgraduate students.

In high-tech areas, cooperative research arrangements with industry are commonplace. Most campuses now find that academic departments divide into the "haves" (technology-related areas) and "have-nots" (humanities and social sciences).

### 2. Tooling and Retooling

With job skills changing at an ever-quickening pace, individuals now make several career changes in a lifetime, and college is still considered the best place for training. Nationwide enrollment has thus fallen only 1.5 percent.

Students are more serious about their studies. Passive acceptance of poor teaching is a relic of the past, and lawsuits by students are common. The implicit view that the professor is somehow superior to the student (left over from the days of in loco parentis) is gone. As students focus almost exclusively on job skills, faculty who prize the liberal arts become a minority.

### 3. Youth Reject Schooling

The plummeting economy makes structural unemployment a

department. In addition, agreement on a "time horizon" is necessary. Because many colleges and universities depend heavily on enrollment for income, the time horizon might be 15 years, a foreseeable horizon with regard to college attendance rates, students' demographic characteristics, and composition of the faculty.

Scenario development is essentially a process of selecting from the total environment those external and internal elements most relevant to the purpose of the strategic plan. This process might well embrace information on demo-

reality. With fewer job openings that require a college degree, all but the most elite youth reject formal schooling. Most young people, weaned on fast-paced information with instant feedback, come to find college teaching methods archaic.

Student bodies are smaller and more homogeneous, comprised mainly of those who can afford the high cost of postsecondary education. A spirit of elitism grows on campus. Among faculty, the mood is one of "minding the store" while waiting for better days.

### 4. Long-Term Malaise

The long-awaited enrollment decline hits, with full force, and the advent of lifelong learning never materializes. The slumping economy forces the states to make deeper funding cuts and close some public campuses.

Faculty attention is focused on fighting closure, and little discussion of programmatic change is evident. Feeling themselves under increasing pressure, many of the best faculty flee the academy. Higher education becomes a shrunken image of its former self.

### 5. A New Industry Is Born

High technology creates a burgeoning demand for job skills. To meet the new challenge, some professional schools break away from their parent university to set up independent institutions. Private corporations establish larger training programs. Even individuals now hang out a shingle and offer educational training. Amid this explosion of new educational forms, the traditional research university breaks down. Community colleges flourish as they adapt to the new needs of the educational market.

Source: Richard Heydinger, cited in *Administrator* 3 (1): 2–3.

graphic characteristics of students, legislative appropriations, research contracts, the health of the economy, public opinion (about the value of a college degree, for example), developments in the field of information processing and telecommunications, and so on.

Furthermore, assumptions about the behavior of a particular variable in a particular scenario must be explicated. Thus, if the size and composition of the 18- to 20-year-old cohort were the variable under consideration, different assumptions might be developed vis-à-vis college attendance rates. One scenario, for example, might assume that in 1995 the number of students in attendance would be the same as in 1983 but that the number of students in the 25- to 45-year-old group would equal the number of students in the 18- to 24-year-old group. An alternative scenario might assume that the number of students would increase by 1995 and that most of them would be third-generation students in the 18- to 21-year-old group. Similar assumptions must be developed for each variable included in the scenario.

Explicating these assumptions is the most important part of creating scenarios and can require a good deal of prior research or, in the case of genius forecast scenarios, great experience, knowledge, and imagination. Once the assumptions are established, however, the nature of each scenario is established. Accordingly, to ensure that they are credible within the institution, it may be worthwhile to review them with local experts. For example, for key factors concerning students, the admissions office might be consulted. For economic variables, the economics department should be consulted. Such consultations are likely not only to improve the quality of the final products but also to build "ownership" into the scenarios, thereby enhancing the chances that they will be considered reasonable possibilities throughout the institution.

In addition to their other advantages, multiple scenarios force those involved in planning to put aside personal perspectives and to consider the possibility of other futures predicated on value sets that may not otherwise be articulated. Grappling with different scenarios also compels the user to deal explicitly with the cause-and-effect relationships of selected events and trends. Thus, multiple scenarios give a primary role to human judgment, the most useful and least well used factor in the planning process. Scenarios therefore provide a useful context in which planning discussions may take place and provide those within the college or university a shared frame of reference concerning the future.[4]

4See Heydinger and Zentner (1983) for a more complete discussion of multiple scenario analysis; see also Boucher and Ralston (1983) and Hawken, Ogilvy, and Schwartz (1982) for a more detailed discussion of the types and uses of scenarios.

**Goal Setting**

Some years ago, in what was apparently the first serious attempt to understand the range and severity of difficulties that face long-range planners, UCLA's George Steiner surveyed real-world experiences in U.S. corporations (Steiner 1972). Steiner's questionnaire, which was completed by 215 executives in large corporations (typically, long-range planners themselves), presented a list of 50 possible planning pitfalls, invited the respondents to suggest others, and then asked three basic questions for each: (1) How would you rank the pitfalls by importance? (2) Has your own corporation recently fallen into any of the pitfalls, partly or completely? (3) If it has, how great an impact has the pitfall had on the effectiveness of long-range planning in your company?

Steiner used the answers from the first question—a more or less global assessment of the influence of the pitfalls on long-range planning—to rank order the items. He did not, however, exploit the much more interesting information about *actual* experience revealed by the answers to the second and third questions. Fortunately, he published the raw data in an appendix. An analysis of those data produces a very different picture of the obstacles to effective planning than does his rank-ordered list. If, for example, one looks for the pitfalls that the largest percentage of companies confess they have recently encountered, "partly" or "completely," the top 10 items are those shown in figure 15. This list is most instructive for planners in all types of organizations, including educational institutions, but seven of these 10 items did not appear anywhere among Steiner's top 10!

Far more significant, however, are the results from the third question, which asked the impact of the pitfalls on the effectiveness of the organization's long-range planning. After all, some mistakes or barriers are more serious than others. If one ranks all of the pitfalls on the basis of the frequency with which real-world planners cited them as having great negative impacts on their effectiveness, another list of the top items emerges (see figure 16). Again, the list is different from Steiner's, but this time five of his candidates appear.

The results for pitfall 28 clearly underscore the importance of appropriate goal setting in an organization. Not

## FIGURE 15
## THE TEN PLANNING PITFALLS MOST COMMONLY FALLEN INTO BY THE LARGEST PERCENTAGE OF CORPORATIONS: RESULTS FROM A SURVEY

| Pitfall Number | Pitfall | Percentage of Corporations | Rank |
|---|---|---|---|
| 49 | Failing to encourage managers to do good long-range planning by basing rewards solely on short-range performance measures. | 82 | 1 |
| 16 | Failing to make sure that top management and major line officers really understand the nature of long-range planning and what it will accomplish for them and the company. | 78 | 2–4 |
| 24 | Becoming so engrossed in current problems that top management spends insufficient time on long-range planning, and the process becomes discredited among other managers and staff. | 78 | 2–4 |
| 47 | Failing to use plans as standards for measuring managers' performance. | 78 | 2–4 |
| 31 | Failing to make realistic plans (as the result, for example, of overoptimism and/or overcautiousness). | 74 | 5 |
| 50 | Failing to exploit the fact that formal planning is a managerial process that can be used to improve managers' capabilities throughout a company. | 71 | 6 |
| 10 | Failing to develop a clear understanding of the long-range planning procedure before the process is actually undertaken. | 69 | 7 |
| 28 | Failing to develop company goals suitable as a basis for formulating long-range plans. | 67 | 8 |
| 37 | Doing long-range planning periodically and forgetting it between cycles. | 65 | 9–10 |
| 39 | Failing, on the part of top management and/or the planning staff, to give departments and divisions sufficient information and guidance (for example, top management's interests, environmental projections, etc.). | 65 | 9–10 |

Source: Steiner 1972.

# FIGURE 16
## THE ELEVEN PLANNING PITFALLS WITH GREATEST IMPACT ON THE EFFECTIVENESS OF CORPORATE LONG-RANGE PLANNING: RESULTS FROM A SURVEY

| Pitfall Number | Pitfall | Percentage Answering "Much" | Rank |
|---|---|---|---|
| 28 | Failing to develop company goals suitable as a basis for formulating long-range plans. | 43 | 1–2 |
| 42 | Failing, by top management, to review with department and division heads the long-range plans they have developed. | 43 | 1–2 |
| 24 | Becoming so engrossed in current problems that top management spends insufficient time on long-range planning, and the process becomes discredited among other managers and staff. | 40 | 3 |
| 45 | Top management's consistently rejecting the formal planning mechanism by making intuitive decisions that conflict with formal plans. | 37 | 4 |
| 38 | Failing to develop planning capabilities in major operating units. | 36 | 5 |
| 7 | Thinking that a successful corporate plan can be moved from one company to another without change and with equal success. | 35 | 6 |
| 3 | Rejecting formal planning because the system failed in the past to foresee a critical problem and/or did not result in substantive decisions that satisfied top management. | 34 | 7 |
| 49 | Failing to encourage managers to do good long-range planning by basing rewards solely on short-range performance measures. | 34 | 8 |
| 1 | Assuming that top management can delegate the planning function to a planner. | 33 | 9–11 |
| 23 | Assuming that long-range planning is only strategic planning, or just planning for a major product, or simply looking ahead at likely development of a present product (that is, failing to see that comprehensive planning is an integrated managerial system). | 33 | 9–11 |
| 32 | Extrapolating rather than rethinking the entire process in each cycle (that is, if plans are made for 1971 through 1975, adding 1976 in the 1972 cycle rather than redoing all plans from 1972 to 1975). | 33 | 9–11 |

Source: Steiner 1972.

only is failure to do it well one of the most frequently encountered barriers to long-range planning (as indicated in figure 15); it also surfaces at the top of the list of pitfalls that can most debilitate comprehensive planning (as shown in figure 16). Moreover, this finding has a certain face validity, for even if an organization has a good idea of what it wants to be (if, that is, it has what is known in strategic planning as a good "mission statement"), it is exceedingly improbable that its forecasting and planning will be fruitful in the absence of clear, actionable statements about how it will know if it is getting there. Such statements are variously called "goals" or "objectives."

Some confusion surrounds these terms in the planning literature. Most authors assert that objectives are more general than goal statements, that objectives are long range while goals are short range, that objectives are nonquantitative ("to provide students with a thorough grounding in the humanities") while goals are quantitative ("to require each student to complete two years of instruction in English, philosophy, and history"), that objectives are "timeless" statements ("to provide quality education that properly equips each student for his chosen career") while goals are "time-pegged" ("to implement a program of education, career counseling, and placement by 1989 such that at least 60 percent of graduates find employment for which they are qualified by virtue of their education at this institution"), and so on. But other authors argue other positions. This problem of vocabulary is in large part one of hierarchies or levels of discourse, as one person's objective can obviously be another person's goal (see Granger 1964 or Kastens 1976, chap. 9). For purposes of this paper, the terms are used interchangeably to mean simply a broad but nonplatitudinous statement of a fundamental intention or aspiration for an organization, consistent with its mission. Metaphorically, a goal or objective in this sense is like a trend around which the actual performance of the institution is expected to fluctuate as closely as possible.

The purpose of goals is to provide discipline. More specifically, the "objectives for having objectives" include:

- To ensure unanimity of purpose with the organization.
- To provide a basis for the motivation of the organization's resources.

- To develop a basis or standard for allocating an organization's resources.
- To establish a general tone or organizational climate, for example, to suggest a businesslike operation.
- To serve as a focal point for those who can identify with the organization's purpose and direction and as an explication to deter those who cannot from participating further in the organization's activities.
- To facilitate the translation of objectives and goals into a work-breakdown structure involving the assignment of tasks to responsible elements within the organization.
- To provide a specification of organizational purposes and the translation of these purposes into goals (that is, lower-level objectives) in such a way that the cost, time, and performance parameters of the organization's activities can be assessed and controlled (King and Cleland 1978, p. 124).

The last two purposes lead especially to management control systems, such as the Planning-Programming-Budgeting system, Zero-Based Budgeting, and Management by Objectives.

To these ends, goals are necessary for every formal structure within an organization, including temporary task forces. If, for example, futures research itself is recognized as a distinct function, the failure to specify goals adequately can lead the futures researcher to assume that his or her domain includes all possible future states of affairs. But the job then becomes futile; all too often the planner is reduced to rummaging in the future, looking willy-nilly for the hitherto unanticipated but "relevant" possibility (Boucher 1978)

Steiner's surprise that pitfall 28 ranked so high on the list of dangerous pitfalls prompted his asking several respondents why they had given it such prominence. Their answers clarify some of the attributes of an "unsuitable" goal:

- It is too vague to be implemented ("optimize profits" or "establish the best faculty").
- It is excessively optimistic. For example, an educational institution with a total annual budget of $10

million would be deluding itself if it sought to "establish the nation's premier faculty in physics."

- It is clear enough to those on the top level who formulated it, but it provides "insufficient guidance" to those on lower levels.
- Finally, it simply has not been formulated. For example, top management has recognized the need to develop goals for lower levels and lower levels would clearly welcome them, but management has not yet been able to specify goals.

How are goals or objectives developed? The short answer is that because they are about the future, they must at bottom be subjective and judgmental. In many organizations, especially small ones, no formal process is required to capture these judgments: The ultimate goals, at least, are the articulated or unarticulated convictions of the founder or top executives about how the organization is likely to look if everyone works intelligently to achieve the mission in the years ahead. The absence of a formal goal-setting process need not mean that the organization is doing something wrong. Indeed, for some of the largest and best-run firms in corporate America, it would appear that the presence or absence of such a process apparently does not matter greatly; what matters more is that a vision is shared and is regularly reinforced by the key people through direct, persistent contact with everyone else. For these companies, this process is a part of what has been called "Management by Wandering Around"—to discover what employees, customers, suppliers, investors, and other stake holders actually think about the organization and its products or services (Peters 1983). By reinforcing a vision through such contacts, these companies are able to adjust their behavior by comparing their mission, goals, and interim performance toward those goals and then shucking subgoals that are blocking the performance they seek.

No educational institution, to our knowledge, practices Management by Wandering Around. Educational planners and policy makers are more likely to use a formal process for setting goals of some sort, particularly those recommended by business schools for use in strategic planning. The many models available (Granger 1964; Hughes 1965;

King and Cleland 1978; Steiner 1969a) tend to be bad models in at least one respect: Almost without exception they fail to recognize the contribution that futures research itself can make to the process of setting goals. The tendency in the literature—and hence in practice—is to suggest that one should, of course, look ahead at the organization's alternative external and internal environments, but, having done that job, one should then proceed to other, more or less independent things, such as setting goals. But futures research can contribute much to this activity, and it can make this contribution *directly*. Indeed, when futures research is operating in the normative mode, goals or objectives may be its principal output.

The key to exploiting this source of information is for the organization to explicitly establish the *preliminary* statement of goals as *one of the goals of its futures research*. We can make this notion more tangible by a simple example. King and Cleland (1978, p. 148 ff.), among others, recommend a process of goal setting that is based largely on "claimant analysis." In that procedure, each of the organization's claimants, or stake holders, is identified— for a public university or college, for example, they might include the trustees, the faculty, other employees, the students, government on all levels, vendors of one sort or another, competing universities, alumni, the local community, and the general public—and each group's principal "claims" on the organization listed. The claims of students, for example, might include obtaining a quality education, varied extracurricular opportunities, contact with faculty, a good library and computer center, nonbureaucratic administrative support services, and so on. Then, for each such claim, a numerical measure is developed, whether direct or indirect. Although the measures will often be difficult to specify, especially in an enterprise as soft as education, the effort should be made. (For example, the quality of education at an institution can be measured in a variety of indirect ways, from counting the number of applications or the number of dropouts to summing the scores on teacher rating sheets, to tracking the results of outside evaluations of the institution's own schools or departments, to measuring the socioeconomic status of alumni.) Finally, past and current levels of these measures are compared to discern whether the institution has been moving toward fulfilling each claimant's proper expectations. When it *has not,* the institution has found a new objective. When it *has,* the current objective has been sustained or rejustified.

This process—whatever its merits—could be strengthened considerably through futures research. If we know who our claimants have been and are now, it is immediately relevant to ask how the nature and mix of claimants might change in the future—or how it should be made to change. The same is true for the claims they might make. By the same token, having measures of their claims, it is clearly worthwhile to project these measures into the future, perhaps using a technique like Delphi, to see what surprises may lie ahead, including conflicts among forecasted measures. With projections of the measures, it is readily possible to ask about the forces that might upset these projections, using a method like cross-impact analysis. Having these results makes it possible to explore the potential efficacy of alternative strategies. Discovering how these strategies might work can then be the source of insight into the need for new or revised goals—goals that not only are responsive to present conditions but also are likely to provide useful guidance as the future emerges. And all of these considerations could then easily be wrapped up in a small set of scenarios (or planning assumptions), which could serve as a framework for the development of future strategic and operational plans.

### Implementation

Forecasting and goal setting work together to define two alternative futures: the expected future and the desired future. The expected future is one that assumes that things continue as they are. It is the "hands-off" future, in which decision makers do not use their newly acquired information about the future to change it. The desired future is the "hands-on" one, and it assumes that whatever the decision makers decide to do works and works well. In stable environments, the two worlds are the same for complacent administrators. But where stability is vanishing and complacency is much too dangerous (as seems to be the case in education today), management must lead in taking a final active step in the strategic planning process: to establish the policies, programs, and plans to move the organization from the expected future to the desired future.

If forecasting and goal setting have been done rigorously and professionally, much of the information needed to accomplish this stage is already identified. A complete forecast contains the structure, framework, and context in which it was produced so as to enable the user to identify appropriate policy responses (De Jouvenel 1967), which can then be implemented. Bardach (1977), Nakamura and Smallwood (1980), Pressman and Wildavsky (1973), and Williams and Elmore (1976) include excellent discussions of this type.

*Forecasting and goal setting work together to define two alternative futures: the expected future and the desired future.*

### Monitoring

Monitoring is an integral part of environmental scanning and of strategic planning. Although the specific functions of monitoring are different in the two processes, they serve the same purposes—to renew the process cycle.

In many planning models, monitoring constitutes one of the first steps, for it is in this step that areas of study are identified and the indicators descriptive of those areas selected. These indicators are then prepared for analysis through the development of a data bank, which can then be used to display trend lines showing the history of the indicators. For example, if enrollments are the area of concern, it is important to select indicators that have historically shown important enrollment patterns and can be expected to do so in the future. That is, one would collect data containing information about entering students (sex, race, age, aptitude scores, major, high school, and rank in the school's graduating class) and perhaps how these students fared while enrolled (grade point average, graduation pattern, and so on). Furthermore, one might select information concerning characteristics of entering college students in similar institutions or nationally in all institutions so that entering students at one's own institution could be compared with others. Such comparisons are readily available through data gathered by the Cooperative Institutional Research Program, an annual survey of new college freshmen conducted by UCLA and the American Council on Education (Astin et al. 1984) and available directly from ACE or from the National Center for Education Statistics.

In this first role of monitoring, historical information is developed and prepared for analysis. This role depends upon the identification of selected areas for study. In the model described here, the areas for study would be developed around the issues identified from environmental scanning and rated as important during evaluation. Monitoring begins its initial cycle at this point in strategic planning. That is, indicators that describe these prioritized issues are selected and prepared for analysis during forecasting.

A number of criteria determine the selection of variables in this cycle. For example, does the trend describe a historical development related to the issue of concern? Is the trend or variable expected to describe future developments? Are the historical data readily available? Gathering data is expensive, and novel sources of data will introduce errors until new procedures are standardized and understood by those supplying the data.

A primary consideration involves the reliability and accuracy of the data. Several writers have dealt thoroughly with criteria for developing and assessing reliable and valid historical data (see, for example, Adams, Hawkins, and Schroeder 1978 and Halstead 1974), but information contained in variables derived from the data must be independent of other factors that would tend to mislead the analysis. For example, if the issue concerns educational costs, is this measurement independent of inflation?

Finally, history must be sufficient so that the data cover the cycle needed for projections; for example, if one is projecting over 10 years, are 10 years of historical data available on that trend?

The second role of monitoring begins after decision makers have developed goals and alternative strategies to reach those goals and have implemented a specific program to implement policies and strategies to move toward the goals. That is, new data in the area of concern are added for analysis so that managers can determine whether the organization is beginning to move toward its desired future or is continuing to move toward the expected future. For example, if the strategies discussed during implementation to increase liberal arts enrollment were employed, the second cycle of the monitoring stage would involve collecting data on enrollments and comparing "new" data to "old" data. Thus, in effect, monitoring is the stage where the effects of programs, policies, and strategies are estimated. The information thus obtained is again used during forecasting. In this fashion, the planning cycle is iterated.

For the environmental scanning model, the specific techniques of monitoring are a function of where an issue is in the development cycle of issues. For some issues, it may be useful to apply some concepts from the emerging field of issues management.[5] The issues development cycle shown in figure 17 focuses on how issues move from the earliest stages of changing values and emerging social trends through the legislative process to the final stages of federal regulations (Renfro 1982). This model is used to understand the relative development stages of issues and to forecast their likely course of developments. Thus, one can see, for example, how the publication of Rachel Carson's *Silent Spring* led to a social awakening of the problems of environmental pollution, which eventually culminated in the formation of the Environmental Protection Agency in 1970. Similarly, Betty Friedan's *The Feminine Mystique* helped to organize and stimulate the emerging social consciousness of the women's movement.

Championing issues through publications is not a new phenomenon. Upton Sinclair used the technique at the turn of the century to alert the country to the issue of food safety in Chicago's meat packing houses with *The Jungle*. Richard Henry Dana used it in *Two Years before the Mast*, published in 1847, to alert the country to the plight of seamen, whose lives were in many ways similar to those of slaves. Thomas Paine's revolutionary pamphlet, *Common Sense*, may be the earliest use of the technique in this country.

Other key stages in the development of public issues are a defining event, recognition of the name of a national issue, and the formation of a group to campaign about the issue. The early stages have no particular order, but each has been essential for dealing with most recent public issues. For example, the nuclear power issue had everything except a defining event to put it into focus until Three Mile Island. Usually the defining event also gives the issue its

[5]The Issues Management Association was first conceived in 1982 and formally established in 1983 with over 400 members. The major concepts and methods of issues management are still in the experimental and developmental stages.

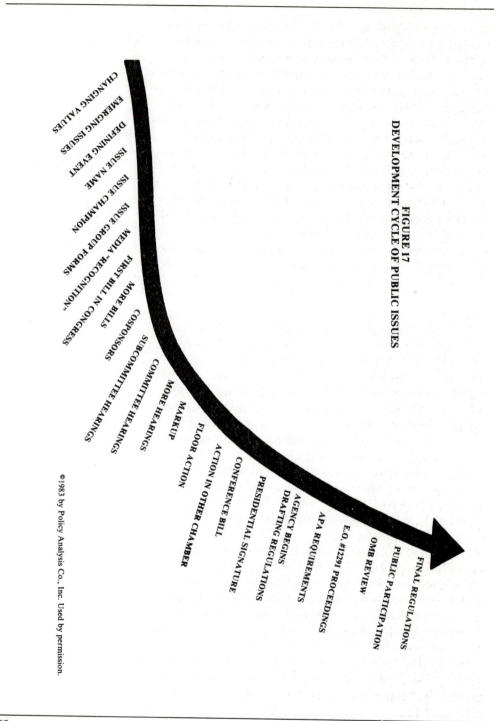

**FIGURE 17**
**DEVELOPMENT CYCLE OF PUBLIC ISSUES**

CHANGING VALUES
EMERGING ISSUES
DEFINING EVENT
ISSUE NAME
ISSUE CHAMPION
ISSUE GROUP FORMS
MEDIA "RECOGNITION"
FIRST BILL IN CONGRESS
MORE BILLS
COSPONSORS
SUBCOMMITTEE HEARINGS
COMMITTEE HEARINGS
MORE HEARINGS
MARKUP
FLOOR ACTION
ACTION IN OTHER CHAMBER
CONFERENCE BILL
PRESIDENTIAL SIGNATURE
DRAFTING REGULATIONS
AGENCY BEGINS
APA REQUIREMENTS
E.O. #12291 PROCEEDINGS
OMB REVIEW
PUBLIC PARTICIPATION
FINAL REGULATIONS

© 1983 by Policy Analysis Co., Inc. Used by permission.

88

name—Love Canal, the DC-10, the Pinto. Of course, all events do not make it through these stages, and many—if not most—are stopped somewhere along the way.

In addition to these general requirements for the development of an issue, several specific additional criteria are needed to achieve recognition by the media: suddenness, clarity, confirmation of preexisting opinions or stereotypes, tragedy or loss, sympathetic persons, randomness, ability to serve to illustrate related or larger issues, the arrogance of powerful institutions for the little guy, good opportunities for photos, and articulate, involved spokesmen. Issues that eventually appear in the national media usually have histories in the regional and local media, where many of the same factors operate (Naisbitt 1982).

At this stage, an issue is or already has been recognized by Congress—recognition being defined by the introduction of at least one bill specifically addressing the issue. Now the issue must compete with many others for priority on the congressional agenda.

For those issues legislated by Congress and signed into law by the president, the regulatory process begins. The basic guidelines for writing new rules are the Administrative Procedures Act (APA) and Executive Order 12291, which require streamlined regulatory procedures, special regulatory impact analyses, and plain language. After the various notices in the *Federal Register,* proposed rules, and official public participation, the regulations may go into effect. This process usually takes three to 10 or more years, making the evolving regulatory environment relatively easy to anticipate using this model and a legislative tracking and forecasting service like Legiscan® or CongresScan™ or following developments in the *Congressional Record.*

This model of the national public issues process is of course continuously evolving. The early stages have shifted from national issues with a single focus to national issues with many local, state, or regional focuses—as the drunk driving, child abuse, spouse abuse, and similar issues demonstrate. The legislative/regulatory process has also been evolving. First, many of the regulations themselves became an issue, especially those dealing with horizontal, social regulation rather than vertical, economic regulation. Regulations for the Clean Air Act, the Equal

Employment Opportunity Commission, the Clean Water Act, the Occupational Safety and Health Administration, the Environmental Protection Agency, and the Federal Trade Commission, among others, have all defined new issues and stimulated the formation of new issue groups, which, like the original issue group, came to Congress for relief. Thus, Congress now is deeply involved in *relegislation* between organized, opposing issue groups—a slow, arduous process with few victories and no heroes.

With Congress stuck in relegislation at such a detailed level so as to itself redraft federal *regulations,* new issues are not moving through Congress. As a result, the list of public issues pending in Congress without resolution continues to grow. Frustrated with congressional delays, issue groups are turning to other forums—the courts, the states, and directly to the regulatory agencies. No doubt the process of recycling issues seen by Congress will emerge here eventually (see figure 18).

The emergence of the states as a major forum for addressing national public issues is not related to new federalism, which is a fundamentally intergovernmental issue. States are taking the lead on a wide range of issues that a decade ago would have been resolved by Congress—the transportation and disposal of hazardous wastes, the right of privacy, the right of workers to know about carcinogens in their work environment, counterfeit drugs, Agent Orange, and noise pollution. The process of anticipating issues among the states requires another model, one focused not on the development of issues across time but across states. In most states, legislators do not have the resources or the experience to draft complicated legislation on major public issues. Moreover, issues tend to be addressed or dropped within one session of the legislative body, and such a hit-or-miss process is almost impossible to forecast. Thus, the legislative ideas from the first state to address an issue are likely to become de facto the national standard for legislation among the other states. The National Conference of State Legislators and the Council of State Governments encourage this cribbing from one state to another, even publishing an annual volume of "Suggested State Legislation." A state legislator need only write in his or her state's name to introduce a bill on a major public issue. The process of forecasting legislative issues across

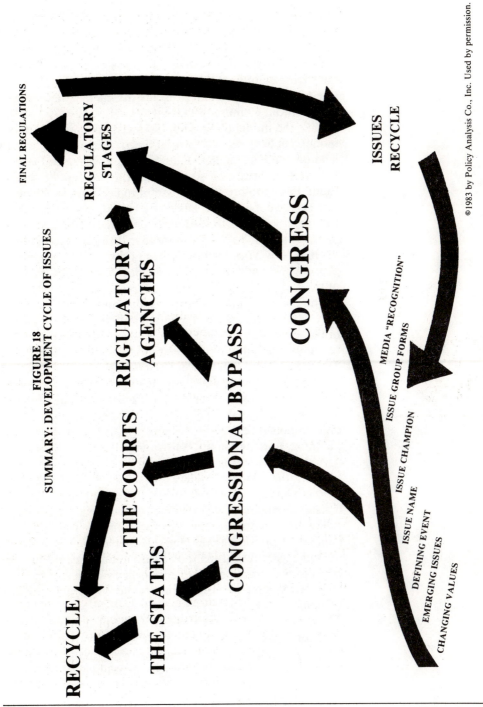

**FIGURE 18**
**SUMMARY: DEVELOPMENT CYCLE OF ISSUES**

FINAL REGULATIONS

REGULATORY STAGES

ISSUES RECYCLE

REGULATORY AGENCIES

THE COURTS

CONGRESSIONAL BYPASS

CONGRESS

MEDIA "RECOGNITION"

ISSUE GROUP FORMS

ISSUE CHAMPION

ISSUE NAME

DEFINING EVENT

EMERGING ISSUES

CHANGING VALUES

RECYCLE

THE STATES

©1983 by Policy Analysis Co., Inc. Used by permission.

the states then involves tracking the number of states that have introduced bills on the issue and the states that have passed or rejected those bills. While the particular language and detailed implementation policies will of course vary from state to state, this model is reasonably descriptive of the process and represents the current state of the art (Henton, Chmura, and Renfro 1984).

Like the model of the national legislative process, this model has been refined several times. Some states tend to lead on some particular issues. While it was once theorized that generic precursor states exist, this concept has been found to be too crude to be useful today. On particular issues, the concept still has some value, however. Oregon, for example, tends to lead on environmental issues; it passed the first bottle bill more than 10 years ago. California and New York lead on issues of taxes, governmental procedures, and administration. Florida leads on the issues of right of privacy.

The piggy-backing of issues is also important. Twenty-two states have passed legislation defining the cessation of brain activity as death. The issue is an important moral and religious one but without substantial impact on its own. Seven states have, however, followed this concept with the concept of a "living will"; that is, a person may authorize the suspension of further medical assistance when brain death is recognized. This piggy-backed issue has tremendous importance for medical costs, social security, estate planning, nursing homes, and so on.

A state forecasting model would be incomplete without another phenomenon, policy cross-over. Occasionally after an issue has been through the entire legislative process, the legislative policy being implemented is reapplied to another related issue without repeating the entire process. The concept of providing minimum electric service to the poor, the elderly, and shut-ins took years to implement, but the concept was reapplied to telephone service in a matter of months. And telephone companies did not foresee the development.

The monitoring stage of the strategic planning process therefore involves tracking not only those variables of traditional interest to long-range planners in higher education (enrollment patterns, for example) but also issues identified through environmental scanning. Moreover, by identifying issues as to where they are in the development cycle of issues, more information is introduced for iteration in the planning process.

# DEVELOPING A STRATEGIC PLANNING CAPABILITY

While the link between environmental scanning and long-range planning is conceptually straightforward, using both within an organization can be complex and confusing, at least initially. This chapter addresses the issues associated with developing a strategic planning process within an existing organization, emphasizing the connection between the scanning function, forecasting/futures research methods, goal setting, implementation, and monitoring. While organizational change can be accomplished from the top down, creating a new function and/or department is often expensive, disruptive, and difficult. More often, successful organizational change is accomplished by more evolutionary processes, in which the new function and/or department grows into being over some period. The process outlined here is focused on this evolutionary growth.

### Early Stages

Strategic planning begins with the selection of a planning model (the one discussed in "The Strategic Planning Process" or another in the wide range of scanning and long-range planning models available for selection). Some of the factors to be considered in the selection of a model of strategic planning include the formality of the model, the resources available within the institution, the size of the institution, available staff and professional resources, and planning requirements imposed on the institution by the external world. The purpose of the model is to provide strategic planning with a structure, a context, and a timetable for producing the plan itself.

An important axiom to remember is that perhaps one of the least important products of the planning process is the plans. Although an obvious overstatement, it serves to underscore the point that the planning process is an ongoing, continuously changing, organic activity. A corollary of the axiom is the perversion of the political axiom, "Plan early and often." The jokes about planned economies stem from the idea that we will today do a 10-year plan and 10 years from now will still be locked into the same plan. Properly understood, however, the strategic planning process creates 10 to 20 or more visions of the interesting future every year. No output of the planning process is ever fixed if its basic assumptions are disrupted.

*The strategic planning process creates 10 to 20 or more visions of the interesting future every year.*

The strategic planning process model has two basic components—the external perspective and the internal perspective. As the intersection of these cycles suggests, the two perspectives overlap, requiring some activities in each to be carried forward concurrently. As most colleges and universities traditionally have had an internal perspective in their long-range planning function, the discussion in the following paragraphs begins with a focus on the external perspective with the intent of merging it with the internal perspective.

An excellent starting place for building an external perspective for an organization is surveying decision makers within the institution to determine several key points: their views of the organization's mission and clientele served, emerging issues in the external world that may affect their responses to the first question, and the kinds of resources they use to stay in touch with this world. A series of informal interviews, which might run 60 to 90 minutes, could accomplish the purpose: Five to 10 decision makers from throughout the institution would be asked to suggest emerging issues of which they are aware and that they believe the institution has not yet begun to address. The request will usually result in five to 10 ideas from each individual interviewed, or from 20 to 30 separate emerging issues potentially important to the future of the institution. Most of the information thus gathered will not be "known" to all those at the institution because of territorial boundaries, crush of daily responsibilities, and immediate fire-fighting requirements. For example, the dean of student affairs may know of an emerging issue in the area of government regulations but have no authority, resources, or incentive to respond or to contact those who do—if they are known.

The second question from this first round of interviews focuses on a survey of the resources administrators use to stay in touch with the external world. The purpose of this survey is to develop a profile of the information resources the senior leadership of the institution currently use to stay in touch with current or emerging issues. Typical results of this survey would show that the information base is narrow—that virtually everyone reads the same thing and that few senior administrators read *Ms., Working Woman, Ebony, Mother Jones,* or *The Futurist.*

In a second round of interviews, the first question changes from identifying the issues to determining how important they are and how likely they are to affect the institution. A simple probability-impact chart could be used for this question. With those issues where there is sufficient consensus, the probability and the impact are multiplied together and the weighted importance thereby determined. The consensus issues are then ranked according to their weighted importance, both positive and negative. The issues for which consensus on either probability or impact is insufficient require additional rounds of discussion and evaluation.

The second question in the process focuses on modifying the resources managers use to stay in touch with the external world. This step takes the form of a simple questionnaire that shows the resources currently scanned and focuses on what additional resources someone in the institution should be reviewing to monitor a particular issue.

The results of this process are not only the improved profile of information resources to be used in the organization and a rank-ordered list of emerging issues but also a growing familiarity within the organization of the concept of environmental scanning. While most organizations resist change imposed on them to some degree, they are less likely to resist—or may even seek—change resulting from their own initiative. The evolutionary, open process of consulting the major decision makers within the institution that systematically produces understandable qualitative and quantitative results provides a most successful way of introducing the idea of environmental scanning in the organization.

The substantive results of the issues evaluation—that is, a rank-ordered list of important emerging issues—provide the basis for the planning assumptions of the external environment for the forecasting stage in the internal perspective. This stage in the process is where the two perspectives first intercept. A simple procedure for evaluating the interaction of these external events on the internal forecasting is an impact chart with the various trends being forecasted for the internal perspective on the vertical axis and the various emerging issues on the horizontal axis. This matrix can be incorporated in a Delphi questionnaire for evaluation by the panel of respondents used in the preceding steps. The question at this point is, on a scale of one to ten, how important each emerging issue is to each one of the components being forecasted for the internal perspective. For example, the trends from the internal perspective might include the number of students, the enrollment mix (science versus liberal arts), labor costs, median faculty salary, percentage of graduate students, percentage of federal aid to the institution, and so on. AT&T before its breakup, for example, produced a set of environmental planning assumptions for use by its member telephone companies in their internal planning. While the member companies were not required to use the parent corporation's planning assumptions, they were required to articulate whatever planning assumptions they used. When a member company used alternative planning assumptions, the alternatives were automatically included in the environmental scanning process of the corporation for its consideration in developing the planning assumptions for the entire corporation the following year. This example highlights the advisory nature of the results produced by scanning. The scanning group thus has no authorization to impose its particular perspective on any division or function of the institution.

For the issues that emerge as the most important, the next stage is to review the institution's scanning resources and match those most important issues with the resource base being used by administrators. At this point, the focus is to develop a monitoring capability to provide the earliest warning to the institution of any further developments as most important issues. For example, if university management is concerned about the percentage of students needing English as a second language, it may be desirable that one of the periodicals scanned is the magazine, *Demographics*. Again, a simple chart of events versus periodicals can quickly lead to the identification of issues that are not now being monitored. Results of the monitoring, then, are to change the resource base of information flowing to the organization.

When this process has been completed for the first time at an informal level, the cycle is ready to be repeated. By now, the executives who have been interviewed should be aware of a central point for reporting new ideas about the changing external world. They should be invited to continue to report on new or emerging issues again and again. Periodically the process of soliciting and evaluating issues should be repeated—eventually through regularly scheduled meetings in which everyone is "interviewed" at once, thereby saving time for those running the scanning system, decreasing the amount of time the process takes, and making the flow of external information more timely.

Eventually these meetings may evolve into a quasi-formal scanning committee that will meet periodically to review and analyze ideas about emerging issues and forward the most important ones to the formal long-range planners. To explore the issues in more detail than the simple probability-impact chart (pages 31–36), members of the scanning committee may want to use a tool like the impact network (pages 36–40) to develop a sense of the nature and kinds of impacts an event may have. Note that the probability-impact chart provides for an evaluation of both positive and negative impacts. The scanning committee, for example, may want to consider the impact of an event on the institution's individual operations and whether these impacts are positive or negative. The purpose of this step is to provide more information about the nature and context of emerging issues and the possible opportunities and threats they pose.

As the scanning cycle is repeated, the function can become more formal with, for example, organized issues files, which might be based on the categories identified initially.

**Link to Long-Range Planning**
Traditional long-range planning begins with a thorough analysis of the current situation. As time passes, the process of keeping this status report current is known as monitoring. Monitoring produces the kind of information contained in annual reports—numbers of students, capital expenditures, number of faculty members, number of degrees granted, and so on. It provides a history of the institution's key features up to the moment. The focus of long-range planning has been to project this information into the future. But the difficulty with this kind of forecasting lies in the fact that the future fails to cooperate. Sooner or later the extrapolations of the past will be upset by external developments, surprises, and changes. A long-range plan-

ning function might have a dozen or more indicators of institutional performance as the subject of its forecasts, but as long-range planners discovered during the 1970s, these forecasts must be modified by a systematic inclusion of the possibility of surprise developments in the external world. No better method to evaluate change in long-range planning and forecasting can be found than that of calculating the impact of surprise events on trends through the probabilistic forecasting techniques like Monte Carlo and trend impact analysis where events are allowed to happen or not happen according to their probabilities, creating distributions of possible futures. Decision makers can then use these distributions of possible futures to expand their vision of what could happen to the trends they are monitoring and thereby provide the information needed to set institutional goals. Moreover, by using the probabilistic forecasting techniques described earlier, it is possible to obtain a range of forecasts of the impacts that different policies designed to implement these goals would have, thereby facilitating decisions about which policies to implement. Linking internal and external perspectives thus serves to enhance college and university planning.

Thus, the inside perspective was based upon a much more stable society, economy, and overall environment than was to be the case in the 1960s and 1970s. Consequently, forecasters and planners developed methods and concepts to include more and more of the external world in internal forecasting. For example, the method of trend extrapolation was modified to include the effects of "surprise" events from the outside world on trend extrapolations. This new method became trend impact analysis. Cross-impact analysis was developed to explore the interaction and interconnection of events. The concept of systems modeling was modified to include external changes; it became known as probabilistic systems dynamics.

Increased emphasis on taking account of changes in the external world continues today in issues management. That is, issues management reverses the inside-out perspective of traditional forecasting and planning to an outside-in perspective in which developments in the external world redefine the issues on which planning must focus. Implicit in this change is the recognition that external developments may have more influence over the future of an institution than previously thought. Moreover, the allocation of significant resources to external scanning assumes that the external environment of the 1980s and beyond will increase in importance as the pace of change continues—or accelerates.

# THE RELEVANCE OF ENVIRONMENTAL SCANNING AND FORECASTING TO HIGHER EDUCATION

College and university planning has evolved through several major stages (Heydinger 1983). Initially, planning constituted part of the annual budgeting process because any planned change must necessarily be considered in projections of revenues and expenses. Although extreme social, political, and technological trends were considered to some extent, the future was viewed primarily in terms of internal financial considerations. It became apparent, however, that not only was an exclusively financial perspective limiting but so also was the one-year time frame. The next stage expanded the time frame for planning beyond the first year, and as the need for qualification and accountability grew, the specification of institutional goals and objectives became a standard against which programs could be measured. The perspective embodied in this stage was that of a cause-and-effect relationship between specifying an institutional future and implementing plans to allocate resources to reach that future.

As our ability to store and manipulate quantitative information increased with the advent of computer centers and, more recently, personal computers, it became possible to project historical data about external forces and forecast the future. But further experience with planning and forecasting revealed not only that the future is unpredictable but also that the forces and interactions affecting colleges and universities were so complex and dynamic that a new planning system was needed. This system needed to be based on the strengths of the previous stages (the budget cycle, specific organizational goals, and the utility of forecasting), but it was also essential that the organization be much more sensitive to the influence of emerging long-term external trends and unprecedented future events that could affect the organization profoundly unless it has carefully prepared itself well in advance to cope with them. This new stage is the era of advanced, comprehensive, and systematic strategic planning.

As modern strategic planning adds a special emphasis on identifying those forces external to the organization that can affect the attainment of its goals, assessment of the environment becomes an important aspect of organizational planning. It also places much greater emphasis on the need to recognize uncertainty—the necessity to consider a range of possible conditions rather than a single future.

Futures research, intended to provide the tools and perspectives required by planners and decision makers who wished to operate most effectively, has developed in parallel with these changes in thinking. The field of futures research has always been controversial, and many academics doubt its legitimacy, particularly those who have been led to believe that futures research seeks to predict the future (which it does not) or that it is a science (which it is not) or that it will somehow supplement established fields like technological or economic forecasting (which it cannot). The approaches, the techniques, and the very philosophy of futures research have been developed to *augment* the capability of individuals and institutions to deal intelligently with change, especially long-term change. Experimental practitioners are well aware that, in historical perspective, the field is very new and that it has only begun to solve some of the problems it must face to achieve this objective. Major figures in the field (for example, Helmer 1983) note that the discipline is not yet on a solid conceptual foundation, a condition caused in part by steady demands for immediate pragmatic results. The fact that techniques of futures research are based upon using the intuitive judgment of experts and require multidisciplinary perspectives has been particularly troublesome to some who value "hardness" and objectivity. These observers, as well as serious practitioners in the field, have also been disturbed by the fact that some charlatans, dilettantes, and incompetents have associated themselves with the field (though they are steadily being shaken out).

Despite imperfections like these, the techniques of futures research—in responsible hands—can greatly facilitate planning because they are designed to provide as clear an accounting as possible of expected changes in the operating environment for which the plans are being formulated (Helmer 1983). Planning staffs and decision makers can quickly learn and use effectively the techniques described in this volume.

Based on experience with successful strategic forecasting and planning in other organizations—the military, private business, trade and professional associations, for example—merging environmental scanning and forecasting with conventional planning approaches will enhance planning in higher education. Although arguing from analogy is always dangerous, there seems to be no reason why many of the lessons painfully learned in other organizations cannot be transferred into the administration of colleges and universities. In the late 1960s, educational institutions at all levels were leading in the development and application of the tools and concepts reported here. But strategic forecasting and planning became a subject that is taught, not used, in education. This situation is no longer tolerable, given the developments facing education today.

Many higher education administrators realize that the need for new approaches is growing. When they recognize that they already have a wealth of information about their institutions and about society and that futures methods and techniques like those described here can provide models for structuring and improving the quality of this information, they will be ready to adopt new methods to build their future.

*If we are to respond creatively, we must begin to look beyond our own organizational boundaries and anticipate internal changes brought on by changing external conditions. We must take our early warning signals, combine them with our existing internal data forecasting techniques, and ensure that we tap the wealth of creativity and resourcefulness higher education has to offer* (Heydinger 1983, p. 86).

# APPENDIX A
## JOURNALS FOCUSING ON THE FIELD OF
## HIGHER EDUCATION

AAHE Bulletin
Academe
AGB Reports
Alternative Higher Education: The Journal of Nontraditional
   Studies
American Journal of Pharmaceutical Education
American Scholar
Assessment in Higher Education
Australian Journal of Education
Canadian Journal of Higher Education
CASE Currents
CAUSE/EFFECT
Change
College and University
College Board Review
College Store Journal
Education Policy Bulletin
Educational Record
European Journal of Education
Graduate Woman
Higher Education
Higher Education Review
Improving College and University Teaching
International Journal of Institutional Management in Higher
   Education
Journal of Architectural Education
Journal of College and University Law
Journal of Dental Education
Journal of Education for Social Work
Journal of Higher Education
Journal of Legal Education
Journal of Medical Education
Journal of Optometric Education
Journal of Podiatric Education
Journal of Student Financial Aid
Journal of Tertiary Education and Administration
Journal of the College and University Personnel Association
Journal of the Society of Research Administrators
Journal of Veterinary Medical Education

Modified from a list of journals used by the ERIC Clearinghouse on
Higher Education in its indexing and abstracting articles for the monthly
bibliographic journal, *Current Index of Journals in Education.*

Liberal Education
NACADA Journal
National Forum: Phi Kappa Phi Journal
New Directions for Experiential Learning
New Directions for Higher Education
New Directions for Institutional Advancement
New Directions for Institutional Research
New Universities Quarterly
Planning for Higher Education
Research in Higher Education
The Review of Higher Education
Studies in Higher Education
Teaching at a Distance
University Administration
Vestes

# APPENDIX B
## PUBLICATIONS SCANNED FOR THE
## TRENDS ASSESSMENT PROGRAM,
## AMERICAN COUNCIL OF LIFE INSURANCE

Across the Board
Administrative Management
Advertising Age
Aging
Aging & Work
American Banker
American Bar Association
  Journal
American Demographics
American Health
American Medical News
American Scholar
American Scientist
Architectural Record
Atlantic Monthly
Behavior Today
Brain Mind Bulletin
Brookings Review
Bulletin of Atomic Scientists
Business & Society Review
Business Horizons
The Business Quarterly
Business Week
California Management
  Review
Canadian Business & Science
Center Magazine
Change—Magazine of Higher
  Education
Channels
Christian Science Monitor
Chronicle of Higher Education
CoEvolution Quarterly
Columbia Journalism Review
Daedalus
Datamation
Discover
Dun's Business Monthly
East West Journal
The Economist
Emerging Trends (religious
  issues)
Family Planning Perspectives

Financial Planner
Financial Times
Footnotes to the Future
Forbes
Foreign Affairs
Fortune
Free Lance
Futures
Future Society
The Futurist
The Gerontologist
Harper's
Harvard Business Review
Harvard Medical Letter
Hastings Center Report
High Technology
Humanist
Industry Week
Institute of Noetic Sciences
  Newsletter
In These Times
Journal of Business Strategy
Journal of Communication
Journal of Consumer Affairs
Journal of Contemporary
  Business
Journal of Insurance
Journal of Long Range
  Planning
Journal of Social Issues
Leading Edge
Management World
Medical Economics
Medical World News
Money Magazine
Monthly Labor Review
Mother Jones
Ms.
Nation's Business
New Age
New England Journal of
  Medicine
New Republic

New Scientist
Newsweek
New Times
New York Review of Books
New York Times
Nuclear Times
Off Our Backs
Omni
Personal Computing
Personnel Journal
Policy Studies Review
The Progressive
Psychology Today
Public Interest
Public Opinion
Public Relations Journal
Rain
Resurgence
Rolling Stone
Quest
Saturday Night
Saturday Review
Savvy
Science
Science and Public Policy
Science Digest
Science 82 (83, 84, 85, etc.)
Science News
The Sciences (NY Academy of
  Sciences)

Science Technology & Human
  Values
Scientific American
Sloan Management Review
Smithsonian
Social Policy
Society
Solar Age
Tarrytown Letter
Technology Forecasts
Technology Illustrated
Technology Review
Time
To The Point
Urban Futures Idea Exchange
USA Today
US News & World Report
Vital Speeches of the Day
Wall Street Journal
The Warton
Washington Monthly
What's Next
The Wilson Quarterly
Working Papers for New
  Society
Working Woman
World Future Society Bulletin
World Press Review

# REFERENCES

The ERIC Clearinghouse on Higher Education abstracts and indexes the current literature on higher education for the National Institute of Education's monthly bibliographic journal *Resources in Education*. Most of these publications are available through the ERIC Document Reproduction Service (EDRS). For publications cited in this list of references that are available from EDRS, ordering number and price are included. Readers who wish to order a publication should write to the ERIC Document Reproduction Service, 3900 Wheeler Avenue, Alexandria, Virginia 22304. When ordering, please specify the document number. Documents are available as noted in microfiche (MF) and paper copy (PC). Because prices are subject to change, it is advisable to check the latest issue of *Resources in Education* for current cost based on the number of pages in the publication.

Ackoff, Russel L. 1970. *A Concept of Corporate Planning*. New York: Wiley-Interscience.

———. 1974. *Redesigning the Future*. New York: Wiley-Interscience.

———. 1978. *The Art of Problem Solving*. New York: John Wiley & Sons.

Adams, Charles F., and Mecca, Thomas V. 1980. "Occupational Education: Some Possible Futures." *World Future Society Bulletin* 14:11–18.

Adams, C. R.; Hawkins, R. L.; and Schroeder, R. G. 1978. *A Study of Cost Analysis in Higher Education*, vol. 1. Washington, D.C.: American Council on Education.

Adams, L. A. 1980. "Delphi Forecasting: Future Issues in Grievance Arbitration." *Technological Forecasting and Social Change* 18(2): 151–60.

Aguilar, F. J. 1967. *Scanning the Business Environment*. New York: Macmillan.

Albert, Kenneth K., ed. 1983. *The Strategic Management Handbook*. New York: McGraw-Hill.

Allen, T. Harrell. Summer 1978. "Cross-Impact Analysis: A Technique for Managing Interdisciplinary Research." *SRA Journal:* 11–18.

Alm, Kent G.; Buhler-Miko, Marina; and Smith, Kurt B. 1978. *A Future Creating Paradigm: A Guide to Long-Range Planning for the Future*. Washington, D.C.: American Association of State Colleges and Universities.

Anderson, Richard E. 1978. "A Financial and Environmental Analysis of Strategic Policy Change at Small Private Colleges." *Journal of Higher Education* 49(1): 30–46.

Ansoff, H. Igor. 1975. "Managing Strategic Surprise by Response to Weak Signals." *California Management Review* 18(2): 21–33.

Armstrong, J. Scott. 1978. *Long-Range Forecasting*. New York: John Wiley & Sons.

Astin, Alexander W.; Green, Kenneth C.; Corn, William S.; and Maier, Mary Jane. 1984. *The American Freshman: National Norms for Fall 1984*. Annual. Los Angeles: UCLA/ACE.

Baier, Kurt, and Rescher, Nicholas, eds. 1969. *Values and the Future: The Impact of Technological Change on American Values*. New York: Free Press.

Baker, Michael. July 1980. "Strategic Long-Range Planning for Universities." Mimeographed. Pittsburgh: Carnegie-Mellon University. ED 189 964. 15 pp. MF–$1.19; PC–$3.74.

Balderston, Frederick. 1974. *Managing Today's University*. San Francisco: Jossey-Bass.

Baldridge, J. Victor, and Okimi, Patricia H. October 1982. "Strategic Planning in Higher Education: New Tool—Or New Gimmick?" *AAHE Bulletin* 35(2): 6, 15–18.

Ball, Ben C., Jr., and Lorange, Peter. 1979. "Managing Your Strategic Responsiveness to the Environment." *Managerial Planning* 28(3): 3–27.

Bardach, Eugene. 1977. *The Implementation Game*. Cambridge, Mass.: MIT Press.

Blackman, A. Wade, Jr. 1973. "A Cross-Impact Model Applicable to Forecasts for Long-Range Planning." *Technological Forecasting and Social Change* 5(3): 233–42.

Boucher, Wayne I. 1972. *Report on a Hypothetical Focused Planning Effort*. Glastonburg, Conn.: The Futures Group.
———. 1978. "Finding the Future: A Practical Guide for Perplexed Managers." *MBA Magazine* 12(7): 48–57.
———. 1984. *Scenarios and Scenario-Writing*. Harbor City, Calif.: ICS Group.

Boucher, Wayne I., and Neufeld, William. 1981. *Projections for the U.S. Consumer Finance Industry to the Year 2000*. Report R-7. Los Angeles: Center for Futures Research, University of Southern California.

Boucher, Wayne I., and Ralston, A. 1983. *Futures for the U.S. Property/Casualty Insurance Industry*. Report R-11. Los Angeles: Center for Futures Research, University of Southern California.

Bourgeois, L. J., III. 1980. "Strategy and Environment: A Conceptual Integration." *Academy of Management Review* 5(1): 25–39.

Bowen, Howard. 1982. *The State of the Nation and the Agenda for Higher Education*. San Francisco: Jossey-Bass.

Bowman, Jim; Dede, Chris; and Kierstead, Fred. November/ December 1977. "Educational Futures: A Reconstructionist Approach." *World Future Society Bulletin* 11: 14–15.

Bracker, Jeffrey. 1980. "The Historical Development of the Strategic Management Concept." *Academy of Management Review* 5(2): 1–24.

Braudel, Fernand. 1972. *The Mediterranean and the Mediterranean World in the Age of Philip II.* Translated by Siân Reynolds. New York: Harper & Row.

Bright, James R. 1978. *Practical Technology Forecasting Concepts and Exercises.* Austin, Texas: Industrial Management Center.

Buhler-Miko, Marina. 1981. "Future Planning and the Sense of Community in Universities." In *The Administrator's Role in Effective Teaching,* edited by Alan Guskin. New Directions for Teaching and Learning No. 5. San Francisco: Jossey-Bass.

Carnegie Council on Policy Studies in Higher Education. 1980. *Three Thousand Futures.* San Francisco: Jossey-Bass. ED 183 076. 175 pp. MF–$1.19; PC not available EDRS.

Cetron, Marvin J. 1969. *Technological Forecasting: A Practical Approach.* New York: Technology Forecasting Institute.

Chaffin, W. W., and Talley, W. 1980. "Individual Stability in Delphi Studies." *Technological Forecasting and Social Change* 16(1): 67–73.

Coates, Joseph F. 1975. "Review of Sackman Report." *Technological Forecasting and Social Change* 7(2): 193–94.

Collazo, A. January 1977. "Forecasting Future Trends in Education." *Educational Leadership* 34: 298 + .

Collier, Douglas. September 1980. "Strategic Planning for Colleges and Universities: The Strategic Academic Unit Approach." Mimeographed. Boulder, Colo.: National Center for Higher Education Management Systems.

———. February 1981. "The Applicability of the Strategic Planning Concept to Colleges and Universities." Mimeographed. Boulder, Colo.: National Center for Higher Education Management Systems.

Cooper, R. L. 1978. *Strategic Policy Planning: A Guide for College and University Administrators.* Littleton, Colo.: The Ireland Educational Corporation.

Cope, Robert G. 1981a. "Providing Assessments of the Environment for Strategic Planning." In *Evaluation of Management and Planning Systems,* edited by N. Poulton. New Directions for Institutional Research No. 31. San Francisco: Jossey-Bass.

———. 1981b. *Strategic Planning, Management, and Decision Making*. AAHE-ERIC Higher Education Research Report No. 9. Washington, D.C.: American Association for Higher Education. ED 217 825. 75 pp. MF–$1.19; PC–$7.24.

Cornish, Edward. 1977. *The Study of the Future*. Washington, D.C.: World Future Society.

Cross, K. Patricia. September 1980. "Two Scenarios for Higher Education's Future." *AAHE Bulletin* 33(1): 1–16.

Crossland, Fred. July/August 1980. "Learning to Cope with a Downward Slope." *Change* 12: 18 + .

Cyert, Richard M. 1983. "Foreword." In *Academic Strategy: The Management Revolution in American Higher Education*, by George Keller. Baltimore: Johns Hopkins University Press.

Cyphert, F. R., and Gant, W. L. 1971. "The Delphi Technique: A Case Study." *Phi Delta Kappan* 52 (5): 272–73.

Dalkey, Norman C. 1969. "An Experimental Study of Group Opinion: The Delphi Method." *Futures* 2(3).

De Jouvenel, Bertrand. 1967. *The Art of Conjecture*. New York: Basic Books.

Dodge, B. J., and Clark, R. E. 1977. "Research on the Delphi Technique." *Educational Technology* 17(4): 58–60.

Doyle, Peter, and Lynch, James. December 1976. "Long-Range Planning for Universities." *Long-Range Planning* 9: 39–46.

———. 1979. "A Strategic Model for University Planning." *Journal of the Operational Research Society* 30(6): 603–9.

Dozier, John, et al. 1980. *A Planning Manual for Colleges*. Washington, D.C.: National Association of College and University Business Officers. ED 185 922. 123 pp. MF–$1.19; PC not available EDRS.

Dresch, S. P. 1975. "Demography, Technology, and Higher Education: Toward a Formal Model of Education Adaptation." *Journal of Political Economy* 83(3): 535–69.

Drucker, Peter. 1954. *The Practice of Management*. New York: Harper & Row.

———. 1974. *Management: Tasks, Responsibilities, Practices*. New York: Harper & Row.

———. 1980. *Managing in Turbulent Times*. New York: Harper & Row.

Edrich, H. January 1980. "Keeping a Weather Eye on the Future." *Planning Review* 8: 11–14.

Ellison, Nolan. September 1977. "Strategic Planning." *Community and Junior College Journal* 48: 32–35.

Enzer, Selwyn. 1970. "A Case Study Using Forecasting as a Decision-Making Aid." *Futures* 2(4): 341–62.

————. 1971. "Delphi and Cross-Impact Techniques: An Effective Combination for Systematic Futures Analysis." *Futures* 3(1): 48–61.

————. 1977. "Beyond Bounded Solutions." *Educational Research Quarterly* 1(4): 22–33.

————. 1980a. "INTERAX—An Interactive Model for Studying Future Business Environments: Part 1." *Technological Forecasting and Social Change* 17 (2): 141–59.

————. 1980b. "INTERAX—An Interactive Model for Studying Future Business Environments: Part 2." *Technological Forecasting and Social Change* 17(3): 211–42.

————. 1981. "Exploring Long-Term Business Climates and Strategies with INTERAX." *Futures* 13(6): 468–82.

————. 1983. "New Directions in Futures Methodology." In *Applying Methods and Techniques of Futures Research*, edited by James L. Morrison, William L. Renfro, and Wayne I. Boucher. New Directions for Institutional Research No. 39. San Francisco: Jossey-Bass.

Eppink, D. J. 1981. "Futures Research: Is It Used? *Long-Range Planning* 14(2): 33–36.

Escher, Firmin. 1976. "College of St. Benedict: A Planning Model That Works." In *A Comprehensive Approach to Institutional Development*, edited by William Bergquist and William Shoemaker. New Directions for Higher Education No. 15. San Francisco: Jossey-Bass.

Fahey, Liam; King, William R.; and Narayanan, Vadake K. 1981. "Environmental Scanning and Forecasting in Strategic Planning: The State of the Art." *Long-Range Planning* 14(1): 32–39.

Fendt, Paul F. 1978. "Alternative Futures for Adult and Continuing Education in North Carolina: A Delphi Futures Planning Study." Paper presented at the first meeting of the Education Section of the World Future Society, October, Houston, Texas. ED 162 545. 20 pp. MF–$1.19; PC–$3.74.

Fincher, Cameron. 1982. "What Is Strategic Planning?" *Research in Higher Education* 16(4): 373–76.

Frances, Carol. July/August 1980a. "Apocalyptic vs. Strategic Planning." *Change* 12: 19–44.

————. 1980b. *College Enrollment Trends: Testing the Conventional Wisdom against the Facts.* Washington, D.C.: American Council on Education.

Gaither, Gerald. 1977. "The Imperative to Plan in Higher Education." *North Central Association Quarterly* 52(2): 347–55.

Gideonse, Hendrik D. 1976. "The Contribution of the Futures Perspective to Management: A Case Study." *Educational Planning* 2(3): 21–34.

Glover, R. H., and Holmes, J. 1983. "Assessing the External Environment." In *Using Research for Strategic Planning,* edited by Norman P. Uhl. New Directions for Institutional Research No. 37. San Francisco: Jossey-Bass.

Gordon, T. J. 1968. "New Approaches to Delphi." In *Technological Forecasting for Industry and Government,* edited by J. R. Bright. Englewood Cliffs, N.J.: Prentice-Hall.

———. 1972. "The Current Methods of Futures Research." In *The Futurists,* edited by Alvin Toffler. New York: Random House.

Gordon, T. J., and Hayward, J. 1968. "Initial Experiments with the Cross-Impact Matrix Method of Forecasting." *Futures* 6(2): 100–16.

Gordon, T. J., and Helmer, Olaf. 1964. *Report on a Long-Range Forecasting Study.* P-2982. Santa Monica, Calif.: The Rand Corporation.

Granger, C. H. May/June 1964. "The Hierarchy of Objectives." *Harvard Business Review* 42: 63–74.

Green, John L., Jr. 1976. "Relationship of Strategic Planning and Budgeting to Financial Difficulty and Organizational Climate in Higher Education." Ph.D. dissertation, Rensselaer Polytechnic Institute.

Green, John L.; Nayyar, Devendra; and Ruch, Richard. 1979. *Strategic Planning and Budgeting for Higher Education.* La Jolla, Calif.: J. L. Green & Associates.

Groff, Warren. January 1981a. "Key External Data Required in Strategic Decision Making: A New Role for Management Systems." *Cause/Effect* 4: 28–34.

———. January/February 1981b. "Market Analysis as an Integral Component of Comprehensive Institutional Planning." *The Snowmass Advisory* 2: 1–11.

———. 1981c. "Market Analysis: What Is It? How Does It Fit into Comprehensive Institutional Planning?" Conference paper prepared for the National Center for Research in Vocational Education. ED 201 343. 56 pp. MF–$1.19; PC–$7.24.

Hackett, E. Raymond, and Morrison, James L. 1981. "Policy Impact Analysis: An Approach to Planning and Budgeting in Higher Education." In *Higher Education Planning and Budgeting: Ideas for the 80's,* edited by M. E. Christal. Boulder, Colo.: National Center for Higher Education Management Systems.

Halstead, Kent. 1974. *Statewide Planning in Higher Education.* Washington, D.C.: U.S. Government Printing Office. ED 096 914. 836 pp. MF–$2.13; PC–$71.90.

Hartman, A. 1981. "Reaching Consensus Using the Delphi Technique." *Educational Leadership* 38(6): 495–97.

Hawken, P.; Ogilvy, J.; and Schwartz, P. 1982. *Seven Tomorrows*. New York: Bantam.

Hearn, James C., and Heydinger, Richard B. In press. "Scanning the External Environment of a University: Objectives, Constraints, and Possibilities." *Journal of Higher Education*.

Hegarty, W. H. September 1981. "Strategic Planning in the 1980s: Coping with Complex External Forces." *Planning Review* 9: 8–12.

Helmer, Olaf. 1966. *Social Technology*. New York: Basic Books.

———. 1975. "Foreword." In *The Delphi Method: Techniques and Applications,* edited by H. Linstone and M. Turoff. Reading, Mass.: Addison-Wesley Publishing Co.

———. 1983. *Looking Forward: A Guide to Futures Research*. Beverly Hills, Calif.: Sage Publications.

Henckley, Stephen P., and Yates, James R. 1974. *Futurism in Education: Methodologies*. Berkeley, Calif.: McCutchan Publishing Corp.

Henton, Douglas C.; Chmura, Thomas J.; and Renfro, William L. 1984. *State Government Issues for Business*. Business Intelligence Program, SRI International.

Heydinger, Richard B. 1983. "The Development of Institutional Research and Planning: Is Futurism the Next Step?" In *Applying Methods and Techniques of Futures Research,* edited by James L. Morrison, William L. Renfro, and Wayne I. Boucher. New Directions for Institutional Research No. 39. San Francisco: Jossey-Bass.

Heydinger, Richard B., and Zentner, Rene D. 1983. "Multiple Scenario Analysis as a Tool for Introducing Uncertainty into the Planning Process." In *Applying Methods and Techniques of Futures Research,* edited by James L. Morrison, William L. Renfro, and Wayne I. Boucher. New Directions for Institutional Research No. 39. San Francisco: Jossey-Bass.

Hofer, Charles W. Spring/Summer 1976. "Research on Strategic Planning: A Survey of Past Studies and Suggestions for Future Efforts." *Journal of Business and Economics* 28: 261–86.

Hofer, Charles W., and Schendel, Dan. 1978. *Strategy Formulation: Analytical Concepts*. St. Paul, Minn.: West Publishing Co.

Hollowood, James R. 1979. *College and University Strategic Planning: A Methodological Approach*. Cambridge, Mass.: Arthur D. Little. ED 181 965. 34 pp. MF–$1.19; PC–$5.49.

Horner, David G. 1979. "Strategic Planning for Higher Education." In *Management Focus*. San Francisco: Peat, Marwick, Mitchell & Co.

Huckfeldt, V. 1972. *A Forecast of Changes in Postsecondary Education*. Boulder, Colo.: Western Interstate Commission for Higher Education. ED 074 919. 215 pp. MF–$1.19; PC–$18.51.

Huckfeldt, V., and Judd, R. C. 1975. *Methods for Large-Scale Delphi Studies*. Boulder, Colo.: National Center for Higher Education Management Systems.

Hudspeth, D. R. 1970. *A Long-Range Planning Tool for Education: The Focus Delphi*. Syracuse: Syracuse University Research Institute.

Hughes, C. L. 1965. *Goal Setting*. New York: AMACOM.

Jamison, David, and Warren, James. 1980. "Forces and Trends Affecting the Future: 1980–1990." Paper read at the American Society for Training and Development National Conference, April 28, Anaheim, California.

Jantsch, E. 1967. *Technological Forecasting in Perspective*. Paris: Organization for Economic Cooperation and Development.

Jedamus, Paul, and Peterson, Marvin W. 1980. *Improving Academic Management*. San Francisco: Jossey-Bass.

Jones, Martin V. 1971. *A Technology Assessment Methodology: Some Basic Propositions*. Washington, D.C.: The MITRE Corp.

Judd, R. C. 1972. "Delphi Applications for Decision Making." *Planning and Changing* 2(2): 151–56.

Judel, Robert C. July 1972. "Forecasting to Consensus Gathering: Delphi Grows Up to College Needs." *College and University Business* 53: 35–38 +.

Kahn, H.; Brown, W.; and Martel, L. 1976. *The Next 200 Years*. New York: William Morrow.

Kane, J. 1972. "A Primer for a New Cross-Impact Language—KSIM." *Technological Forecasting and Social Change* 4(2): 129–42.

Kast, F. Fall 1980. "Scanning the Future Environment: Social Indicators." *California Management Review* 23: 22–32.

Kastens, Merritt L. 1976. *Long-Range Planning for Your Business*. New York: AMACOM.

Keller, George. 1983. *Academic Strategy: The Management Revolution in American Higher Education*. Baltimore: Johns Hopkins University Press.

King, William R., and Cleland, David I. 1978. *Strategic Planning and Policy*. New York: Van Nostrand Reinhold Co.

Kirschling, W., and Huckfeldt, V. 1980. "Projecting Alternative Futures." In *Improving Academic Management*, edited by Paul Jedamus and Marvin Peterson. San Francisco: Jossey-Bass.

Klein, H. E., and Linneman, R. 1981. "The Use of Scenarios in Corporate Planning—Eight Case Histories." *Long-Range Planning* 14(5): 69–77.

Klein, H. E., and Newman, W. H. July 1980. "How to Integrate New Environmental Forces into Strategic Planning." *Management Review* 69: 40–48.

Lindberg, R. A. 1979. *Long-Range Planning.* New York: American Management Association.

Linneman, R. E., and Klein, H. E. 1979. "The Use of Multiple Scenarios by U. S. Industrial Companies." *Long-Range Planning* 12(1): 83–90.

Linstone, Harold A. 1972. "Four American Futures: Reflections on the Role of Planning." *Technological Forecasting and Social Change* 4(1): 41–60.

———. 1983. "Book Review." *Technological Forecasting and Social Change* 24(2): 178–79.

Linstone, Harold A., and Simmonds, W. H., eds. 1977. *Futures Research: New Directions.* Reading, Mass.: Addison-Wesley.

Linstone, H. A., and Turoff, M., eds. 1975. *The Delphi Method: Techniques and Applications.* Reading Mass.: Addison-Wesley.

Locatis, C. N., and Gooler, D. D. Spring 1975. "Evaluating Second-order Consequences: Technology Assessment and Education." *Review of Education Research* 45: 327–53.

Lonsdale, Richard C. 1975. "Futures Research, Policy Research, and the Policy Sciences." *Education and Urban Society* 7(3): 246–93.

McLaughlin, Curtis P. Winter 1976. "Strategic Planning and Control in Small Health Organizations." *Health Care Management Review* 1: 45–53.

———. Summer 1982. "Strategic Planning under Current Cutback Conditions." *Health Care Management Review* 7: 7–17.

———. 1984. *Leadership and Management in Academic Medical Centers.* San Francisco: Jossey-Bass.

McNamara, J. F. December 1971. "Mathematical Programming Models in Educational Planning." *Review of Educational Research* 41: 419–46.

MacNow, Glen. 18 May 1983. "Michigan to Study State Colleges; Some Could Shift." *Chronicle of Higher Education* 26(12): 1 + .

Manchester, William R. 1974. *The Glory and the Dream: A Narrative History of America, 1932–1972.* Boston: Little, Brown.

Mandel, T. F. 1983. "Futures Scenarios and Their Uses in Corporate Strategy." In *The Strategic Management Handbook,* edited by Kenneth K. Albert. New York: McGraw-Hill.

Marien, Michael, and Ziegler, Warren L., eds. 1972. *The Potential of Educational Futures*. Worthington, Ohio: Charles A. Jones (for the National Society for the Study of Education).

Martino, Joseph. 1970. "The Precision of Delphi Estimates." *Technological Forecasting and Social Change* 1(3): 293–99.
————.1972. *An Introduction to Technological Forecasting*. New York: Gordon & Breach.

Meadows, D. H.; Meadows, D. L.; Randers, J.; and Behrens, W. W., III. 1972. *The Limits to Growth: A Report for the Club of Rome's Project on the Predicament of Mankind*. New York: Universe Books.

Mecca, Thomas V., and Adams, Charles F. May/June 1982. "ED QUEST: An Environmental Scanning Process for Education Agencies." *World Future Society Bulletin* 16: 7–12.

Merson, John, and Qualls, Robert. 1979. *Strategic Planning for Colleges and Universities*. San Antonio: Trinity University Press.

Michael, D. 1973. *On Learning to Plan and Planning to Learn*. San Francisco: Jossey-Bass.

Mitchell, R. B.; Tydeman, J.; and Curnon, R. 1977. "Scenario Generation: Limitations and Developments in Cross-Impact Analysis." *Futures* 9: 205–15.

Morgan, A. W. 1983. "Cost as a Policy Issue: Lessons for the Health Care Sector." *Journal of Higher Education* 54(3): 279–93.

Morrison, James L. 1980. *Annotated Bibliography of Literature on Social Indicators, Future Studies, and Policy Analysis*. Technical Report 509. Alexandria, Va.: U. S. Army Research Institute for the Behavioral and Social Sciences.
————. 1981a. "Policy Impact Analysis: Implications for Use with Regional Data Bases on Social/Educational Indicators." In *Visions, Issues, and Reality: A Changing South*, edited by B. H. Willis. Research Triangle Park, N.C.: Southeastern Regional Council for Educational Improvement.
————. 1981b. "Policy Impact Analysis: Rational Method to Respond to the Challenges Faced by Higher Education in the Eighties." Mimeographed. Paper presented at the Florida State University Institute for Studies in Higher Education, May 5. ED 201 292. 18 pp. MF–$1.19; PC–$3.74.

Morrison, James L.; Renfro, William L.; and Boucher, Wayne I., eds. 1983. *Applying Methods and Techniques of Futures Research*. New Directions for Institutional Research No. 39. San Francisco: Jossey-Bass.

Munger, Frank J., and Morrison, James L. 1981. "Designing a Regional Data Base for Futures Research in Educational Policy Making." *University of North Carolina Newsletter* 66(1): 14–15.

Nadelson, C. February 1983. "Emerging Issues for College Students in the 1980s." *Journal of American College Health* 31: 177–84.

Nair, Keshavan, and Sarin, Rakesh. 1979. "Generating Future Scenarios: Their Use in Strategic Planning." *Long-Range Planning* 12(3): 57–61.

Naisbitt, John. 1982. *Megatrends*. New York: Warner Books.

Nakamura, Robert T., and Smallwood, Frank. 1980. *The Politics of Policy Implementation*. New York: St. Martin's Press.

Nanus, B. 1982. "QUEST—Quick Environmental Scanning Technique." *Long-Range Planning* 15(2): 39–45.

Nash, Nicholas. 1978. "Delphi and Educational Research: A Review." ED 151 950. 55 pp. MF–$1.19; PC–$7.24.

Naylor, M. E. 1983. "Planning for Uncertainty—The Scenario-Strategy Matrix." In *The Strategic Management Handbook*, edited by Kenneth K. Albert. New York: McGraw-Hill.

Ogburn, William F. 1933. *Recent Social Trends in the United States*. New York: McGraw-Hill.

Parekh, Satish B. 1975. *Long-Range Planning: An Institution-Wide Approach to Increasing Academic Vitality*. New Rochelle, N.Y.: Change Magazine Press.

Patterson, Franklin. August 1977. "Institutional Planning in the Context of Change." *Planning for Higher Education* 6: 1–8.

Peters, Thomas J. Spring 1983. "We Underestimated: Excellent Companies Revisited."*New Management:* 6–11.

Peterson, Marvin W. 1980. "Analyzing Alternative Approaches to Planning." In *Improving Academic Management*, edited by Paul Jedamus and Marvin W. Peterson. San Francisco: Jossey-Bass.

Pfnister, Allan O. 1976. *Planning for Higher Education: Background and Application*. Boulder, Colo.: Westview Press.

Pressman, Jeffrey, and Wildavsky, Aaron. 1973. *Implementation*. Berkeley: University of California Press.

Pyke, Donald L. June 1970. "A Practical Approach to Delphi." *Futures* 2(2): 143–52.

———. 1971. "Mapping—A System Concept for Displaying Alternatives." *Technological Forecasting and Social Change*. 2(3–4): 311–20.

Quinn, James Brian. Summer 1980. "Managing Strategic Change." *Sloan Management Review* 21: 3–20.

Radford, K. J. 1980. *Strategic Planning: An Analytical Approach*. Reston, Va.: Reston Publishing Co.

Rasp, Alfred F. 1974. "Delphi: A Strategy for Decision Implication." *Educational Planning* 1(2): 42–47.

Reeves, G., and Jauch, L. R. 1971. "Curriculum Development through Delphi." *Research in Higher Education* 8(2): 157–68.

Renfro, W. L. August 1980a. "Congress, Corporations, and Crystal Balls: A Partnership for the Future?" *Planning Review* 8: 36–42.

———. August 1980b. "Forecasting the Impact of Public Policies. *Long-Range Planning* 13: 80–89.

———. 1980c. "Policy Impact Analysis: A Third Generation Approach." *World Future Society Bulletin* 14(4): 19–26.

———. August 1982. "Managing the Issues of the 1980s." *The Futurist* 16: 61–66.

Renfro, William L., and Morrison, James L. October 1982. "Merging Two Futures Concepts: Application to Educational Policy." *The Futurist* 16: 54–56.

———. 1983a. "Anticipating and Managing Change in Educational Organizations." *Educational Leadership* 41(1): 50–54.

———. August 1983b. "Scanning the External Environment: Organizational Issues." In *Applying Methods and Techniques of Futures Research,* edited by James L. Morrison, William L. Renfro, and Wayne I. Boucher. New Directions for Institutional Research No. 39. San Francisco: Jossey-Bass.

———. 1984. "Detecting Signals of Change: The Environmental Scanning Process." *The Futurist* 18(4): 49–56.

———. 1985. *The Delphi Decision Support System: Making the Technique Work*. Washington, D.C.: Policy Analysis Co., Inc.

Rochberg, Richard; Gordon, Theodore J.; and Helmer, Olaf. 1970. *The Use of Cross-Impact Matrices for Forecasting and Planning*. Middletown, Conn.: Institute for the Future.

Rosove, Perry E. 1968. *An Analysis of Possible Future Roles of Educators as Derived from a Contextual Map*. Santa Monica, Calif.: System Development Corporation.

Rossman, M. H., and Bunning, R. L. 1978. "Knowledge and Skills for the Adult Educator: A Delphi Study." *Adult Education* 28(3): 139–55.

Rubin, Louis, ed. 1975. *The Future of Education: Perspectives on Tomorrow's Schooling*. Boston: Allyn & Bacon.

Sackman, H. 1975. *Delphi Critique*. Lexington, Mass.: D.C. Heath.

Salancik, J.R. 1973. "Assimilation of Aggregated Inputs into Delphi Forecasts: A Regression Analysis." *Technological Forecasting and Social Change* 5(3): 243–48.

Salancik, J. R.; Wenger W.; and Helfer, E. 1971. "The Construction of Delphi Event Statements." *Technological Forecasting and Social Change* 3(1): 65–73.

Schendel, Dan E., and Hatten, Kenneth J. 1972. "Strategic Planning and Higher Education: Some Concepts, Problems, and Opportunities." Reprint No. 442. Lafayette, Ind.: Institute for Research in the Behavioral, Economic, and Management Sciences, Purdue University.

Scigliano, John A. Winter 1981a. "Strengthening Hope and Purpose in Community College Futures through Strategic Marketing Planning." *Community Services Catalyst* 11: 16–21.

———. 1981b. "A Systems Approach to the Design and Operation of Effective Marketing Programs." In *Marketing the Program*, edited by William A. Keim and Marybelle C. Keim. New Directions for Community Colleges No. 36. San Francisco: Jossey-Bass.

Sheehan, Bernard. 1981. "Institutional Planning." In *Higher Education Planning: A Bibliographic Handbook,* edited by Kent Halstead. Washington, D.C.: National Institute of Education.

Shirley, Robert. 1978. "Strategic Decision Making in Colleges and Universities." Paper presented at the annual forum of the Association for Institutional Research, May 21–25, Houston. ED 161 395. 17 pp. MF–$1.19; PC–$3.74.

———. 1983. "Identifying the Levels of Strategy for a College or University." *Long-Range Planning* 16(3): 92–98.

Steiner, George A. 1969a. *Strategic Factors in Business Success.* New York: Macmillan.

———. 1969b. *Top Management Planning.* New York: Macmillan.

———. 1972. *Pitfalls in Comprehensive Long-Range Planning.* Oxford, Ohio: The Planning Executives Institute.

Stubbart, Charles. 1982. "Are Environmental Scanning Units Effective?" *Long-Range Planning* 15(3): 139–45.

Sullivan, William G., and Claycombe, W. Wayne. 1977. *Fundamentals of Forecasting.* Reston, Va.: Reston Publishing Co.

Teddlie, Charles; Hackett, E. Raymond; and Morrison, James L. 1982. "Developing Public Educational Policy through Policy-Impact Analysis." *World Future Society Bulletin* 16(6): 25–30.

Thomas, Raymond. October 1980. "Corporate Strategic Planning in a University." *Long-Range Planning* 13: 70–78.

Uhl, Norman P. 1970. "A Technique for Improving Communication within an Institution." In *Institutional Research and Communication in Higher Education,* edited by P. Wright. Tallahassee: Association of Institutional Research. ED 046 093. 289 pp. MF–$1.19; PC not available EDRS.

————. 1980. "An Action-Oriented Technique for Improving a Campus Environment." In *The Impact of Desegregation on Higher Education,* edited by Jeff Smith. Durham, N.C.: North Carolina Central University Institute on Desegregation.

————, ed. 1983a. *Using Research for Strategic Planning.* New Directions for Institutional Research No. 37. San Francisco: Jossey-Bass.

————. 1983b. "Using the Delphi Technique in Institutional Planning." In *Using Research for Strategic Planning,* edited by Norman P. Uhl. New Directions for Institutional Research No. 37. San Francisco: Jossey-Bass.

U.S. Congress. House Committee on Science and Astronautics. July 1969a. *A Study of Technology Assessment: Report of the Committee on Public Engineering Policy, National Academy of Engineering.* Washington, D.C.: U.S. Government Printing Office.

————. July 1969b. *Technology: Processes of Assessment and Choice: Report of the National Academy of Sciences.* Washington, D.C.: U.S. Government Printing Office.

Vanderwicken, P. 1982. " 'Externalysis': A New Dimension in Planning." *Planning Review* 10(4): 24–27 + .

Wagschall, Peter H. August 1983. "Judgmental Forecasting Techniques and Institutional Planning." In *Applying Methods and Techniques of Futures Research,* edited by James L. Morrison, William L. Renfro, and Wayne I. Boucher. New Directions for Institutional Research No. 39. San Francisco: Jossey-Bass.

Weaver, W. Timothy. June 1970. *The Delphi Method.* Syracuse, N.Y.: Educational Policy Research Center.

————. 1971. "The Delphi Forecasting Method." *Phi Delta Kappan* 52(5): 267–71.

Weiner, E. September/October 1976. "Future Scanning for Trade Groups and Companies." *Harvard Business Review* 54:14 + .

Williams, Charles, and Nusberg, Charlotte. 1973. *Anticipating Educational Issues over the Next Two Decades: An Overview Report of Trends Analysis.* Washington, D.C.: National Center for Educational Research and Development. ED 074 627. 78 pp. MF–$1.19; PC–$9.37.

Williams, Walter, and Elmore, Richard F., eds. 1976. *Social Program Implementation.* New York: Academic Press.

Wissema, J. G. 1981. "Futures Research: Is It Useful?" *Long-Range Planning* 14(2): 33–36.

————. 1982. "The Modern Prophets—How Can They Help Us?" *Long-Range Planning* 15(4): 126–34.

Young, Wanda E. August 1978. "Determination of Educational Policy by Futures Research Methods." ED 161 139. 16 pp. MF–$1.19; PC–$3.74.

Zentner, R. D. 1982. "Scenarios Past, Present, and Future." *Long-Range Planning* 15(3): 12–20.

Ziegler, Warren L. 1970. *An Approach to the Futures Perspective in American Education*. Syracuse, N.Y.: Educational Policy Research Center. ED 046 046. 107 pp. MF–$1.19; PC–$11.12.

# ASHE-ERIC HIGHER EDUCATION RESEARCH REPORTS

Starting in 1983, the Association for the Study of Higher Education assumed cosponsorship of the Higher Education Research Reports with the ERIC Clearinghouse on Higher Education. For the previous 11 years, ERIC and the American Association for Higher Education prepared and published the reports.

Each report is the definitive analysis of a tough higher education problem, based on a thorough research of pertinent literature and institutional experiences. Report topics, identified by a national survey, are written by noted practitioners and scholars with prepublication manuscript reviews by experts.

Ten monographs in the ASHE-ERIC Higher Education Research Report series are published each year, available individually or by subscription. Subscription to 10 issues is $55 regular; $40 for members of AERA, AAHE, and AIR; $35 for members of ASHE. (Add $7.50 outside U.S.)

Prices for single copies, including 4th class postage and handling, are $7.50 regular and $6.00 for members of AERA, AAHE, AIR, and ASHE. If faster 1st class postage is desired for U.S. and Canadian orders, for each publication ordered add $.75; for overseas, add $4.50. For VISA and MasterCard payments, give card number, expiration date, and signature. Orders under $25 must be prepaid. Bulk discounts are available on orders of 10 or more of a single title. Order from the Publications Department, Association for the Study of Higher Education, One Dupont Circle, Suite 630, Washington, D.C. 20036, (202) 296-2597. Write for a complete list of Higher Education Research Reports and other ASHE and ERIC publications.

### 1982 Higher Education Research Reports

1. Rating College Teaching: Criterion Studies of Student Evaluation-of-Instruction Instruments
   *Sidney E. Benton*

2. Faculty Evaluation: The Use of Explicit Criteria for Promotion, Retention, and Tenure
   *Neal Whitman and Elaine Weiss*

3. The Enrollment Crisis: Factors, Actors, and Impacts
   *J. Victor Baldridge, Frank R. Kemerer, and Kenneth C. Green*

4. Improving Instruction: Issues and Alternatives for Higher Education
   *Charles C. Cole, Jr.*

5. Planning for Program Discontinuance: From Default to Design
   *Gerlinda S. Melchiori*

6. State Planning, Budgeting, and Accountability: Approaches for Higher Education
   *Carol E. Floyd*

7. The Process of Change in Higher Education Institutions
   *Robert C. Nordvall*

8. Information Systems and Technological Decisions: A Guide for Non-Technical Administrators
   *Robert L. Bailey*

9. Government Support for Minority Participation in Higher Education
   *Kenneth C. Green*

10. The Department Chair: Professional Development and Role Conflict
    *David B. Booth*

**1983 Higher Education Research Reports**

1. The Path to Excellence: Quality Assurance in Higher Education
   *Laurence R. Marcus, Anita O. Leone, and Edward D. Goldberg*

2. Faculty Recruitment, Retention, and Fair Employment: Obligations and Opportunities
   *John S. Waggaman*

3. Meeting the Challenges: Developing Faculty Careers
   *Michael C. T. Brookes and Katherine L. German*

4. Raising Academic Standards: A Guide to Learning Improvement
   *Ruth Talbott Keimig*

5. Serving Learners at a Distance: A Guide to Program Practices
   *Charles E. Feasley*

6. Competence, Admissions, and Articulation: Returning to the Basics in Higher Education
   *Jean L. Preer*

7. Public Service in Higher Education: Practices and Priorities
   *Patricia H. Crosson*

8. Academic Employment and Retrenchment: Judicial Review and Administrative Action
   *Robert M. Hendrickson and Barbara A. Lee*

9. Burnout: The New Academic Disease
   *Winifred Albizu Meléndez and Rafael M. de Guzmán*

10. Academic Workplace: New Demands, Heightened Tensions
    *Ann E. Austin and Zelda F. Gamson*